# The Fiddlin' Workshop for Cello

I0810739

## Jeanine Orme

Online Audio

To access the online audio go to:
*WWW.MELBAY.COM/30774MEB*

MEL BAY®


*WWW.MELBAY.COM*

# Introduction

This book was written to be used as a learning tool for student cellists who want to play fiddle tunes. While it contains the same tunes in the same keys as the original *The Fiddlin' Workshop* and *The Fiddlin' Workshop for Viola*, many of the arrangements have been modified to make fingering for cello easier with minimal shifting. For some tunes, more than one version is presented. The tunes are written in the typical keys that most fiddlers use. The book presents easy tunes to learn the basics of bowing and style, and progresses in difficulty with each tune.

Fiddle tunes can be played in many different ways, and each fiddler has his or her own interpretation of how a tune should be played. This book provides practical fingerings and bowings for each tune, often with additional information or instruction. Fiddlers can add their own interpretation of slurs, bowing, ornamentation and rhythmic feel to develop their individual style.

# About the Author

Jeanine Rabe Orme began playing the violin at age five and was fiddling by the time she was eight. During her youth she performed with the Utah Old Time Fiddlers, and began entering fiddle contests. She competes regularly at the Weiser National Oldtime Fiddlers' Contest, as well as other state and local contests. She is a past Utah State Fiddle Champion and Oregon State Fiddle Contest Young Adult and Adult Division winner.

Her music was influenced significantly by the late Herman Johnson of Shawnee, Oklahoma. Mr. Johnson instructed her in Texas-style fiddling as well as in the swing fiddle style.

Jeanine has been teaching fiddle lessons for over 40 years and regularly teaches fiddle workshops and camps. She has also played fiddle, bluegrass and swing music with various bands in Utah and Oregon. Jeanine resides in Beaverton, Oregon and is the mother of three adult children.

# Acknowledgements

The audio tracks for this book were performed by Maralyn Smart Belgique. Technical help with the audio tracks was provided by Jon Newton.

1 Tuning Pitch

# Contents

# Overview of Musical Symbols and Style

*sl.* **Slide the finger** - This marking indicates that a slide adds to the style of the song.

[A] **Section marking**

♪ **Grace note** - Ornamental note with no value by itself. Slur quickly into the next note.

X4 **Extended finger** - The finger should be extended an extra half step.

**Triplet** - Grouping of three notes played in the same time allotted to two notes of the same value.

**D. C. al Fine** - Return to the beginning and play until you see the word "*Fine*"

**Double stop** - two notes played at the same time.

Example: 0 4

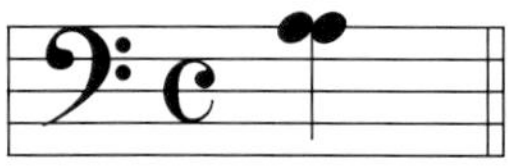

4th finger and open string are played together.

**Fingering** - Finger numbers are indicated when correct fingering makes a difference in the ease of playing or adds to the style of the tune.

**Shifting** - A shift to third or fourth position is marked with correct fingering.

**Guitar Chords** - The guitar chords presented in this collection are basic and functional. Many variations or additional chords could be added.

## Tips on Bowing

1) The wrist of the bow hand should be flexible, not stiff. Use more wrist movement, especially on passages that are fast.

2) In general, start a new phrase with a down-bow to accent the first beat.

3) Use a pattern of three-note slurs instead of two-note slurs. Your bow direction will not change if you add or take away a three-note slur.

**Bowing Interpretation** - The bowing style for this collection is based on a pattern of three-note slurs. When you use a three-note slur, the bow direction does not change. Each phrase usually begins on a down-bow. This style of bowing will generally yield a smooth flow of notes.

Example 1 - Two-note slur pattern:

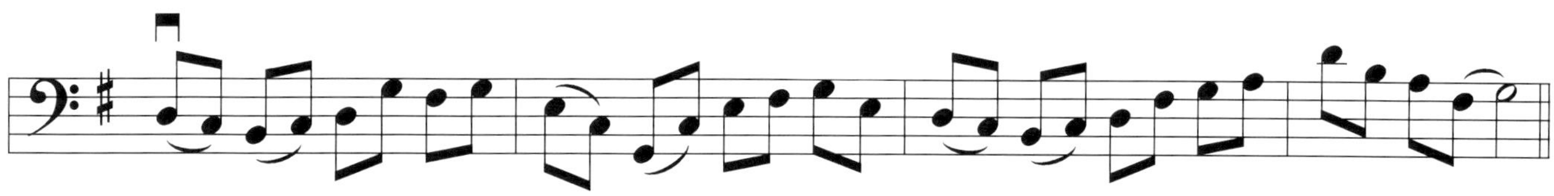

Example 2 - Three-note slur pattern:

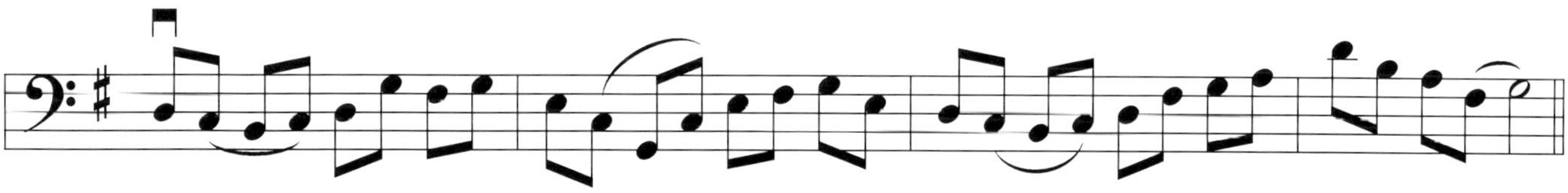

## Developing Swing Rhythm

Many fiddle tunes (including waltzes) should be played with an *implied* swing rhythm of the eighth notes. It is customary to write swing rhythm as "straight eighth" notes, but when "swing rhythm" appears over the first measure, the pairs of 8th notes are played as triplet figures.

Swing rhythm

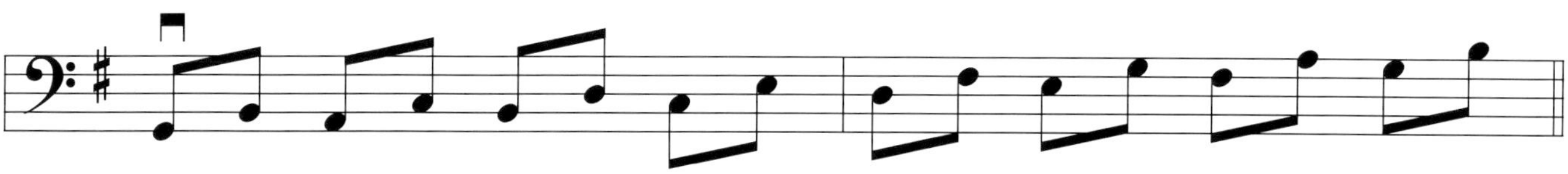

A swing rhythm is *approximated* in the quarter note with eighth-note triplet pattern below:

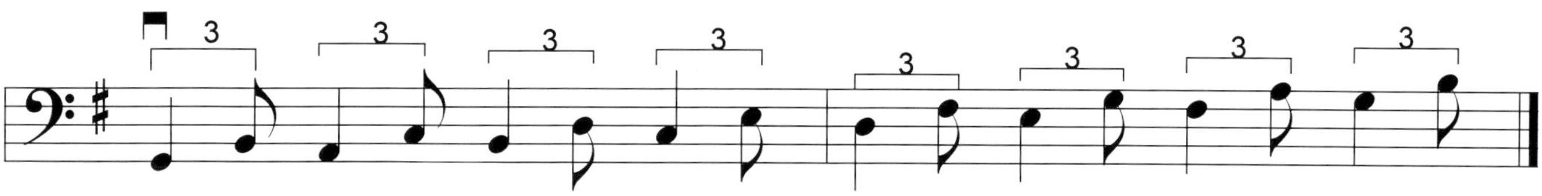

# Scales and Key Signatures

The following major key signatures and scales are used in this book:

C Major-lower octave

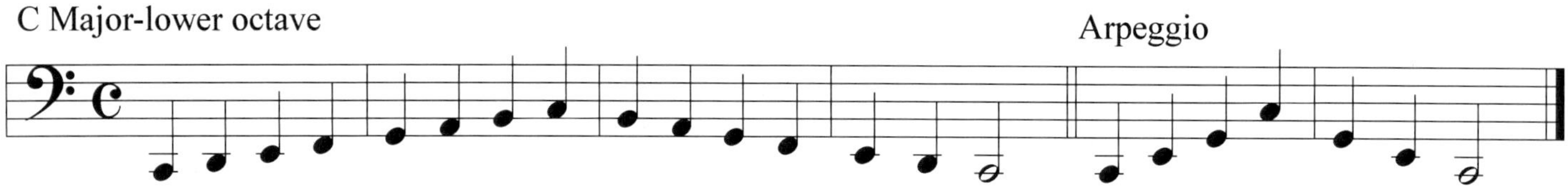


C Major-higher octave

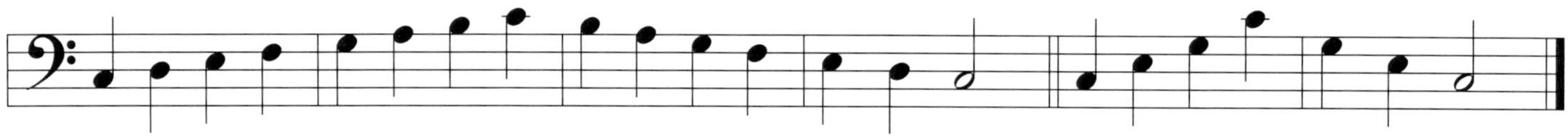

G Major

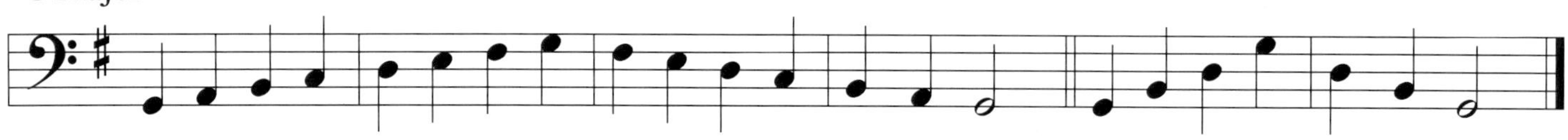

**Introduction to Extended Position:** Extending the hand allows a cellist to play higher notes without shifting. An extended hand position opens the hand one half step larger than a closed position. The second finger is placed where the third finger normally goes. Then, stretch the 4th finger to play the extended 4th-finger note.

D Major-lower octave

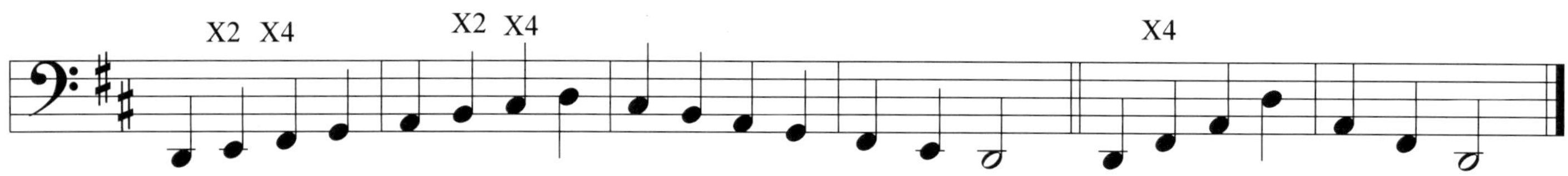


D Major-higher octave

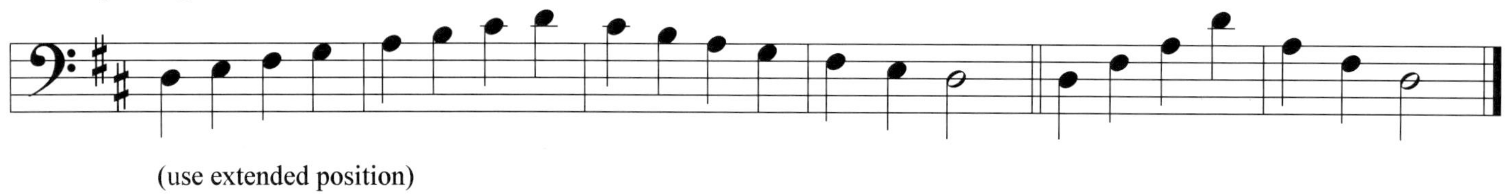


A Major

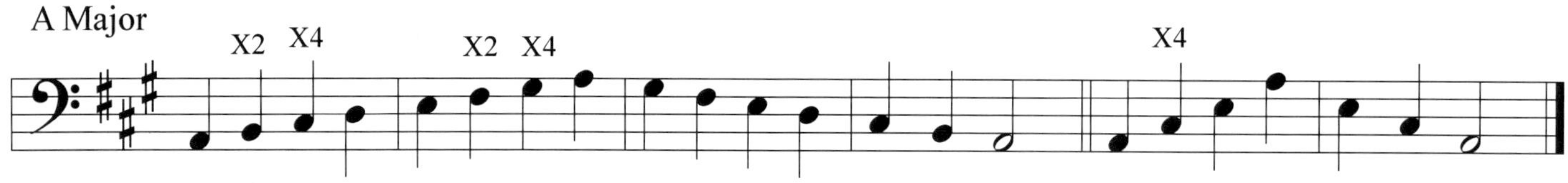


**Introduction to Shifting: Shifting to Fourth Position**
When a shift to a higher note is needed, shift the entire hand to the new location keeping the basic left-hand formation.

F Major

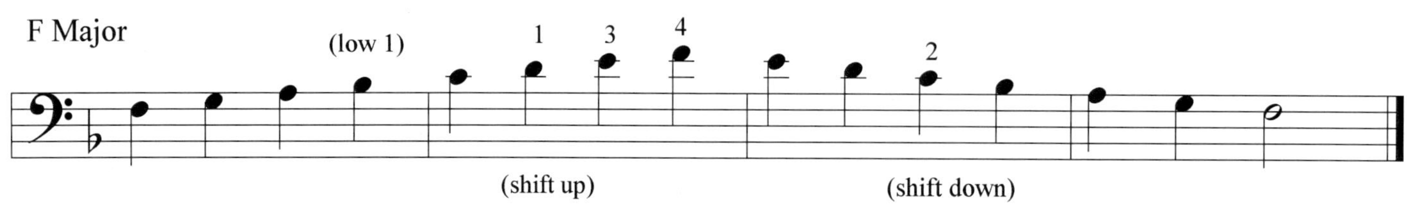

*This page has been left blank to avoid an awkward page turn.*

# Soldier's Joy

Straight rhythm
Fast tempo

Traditional

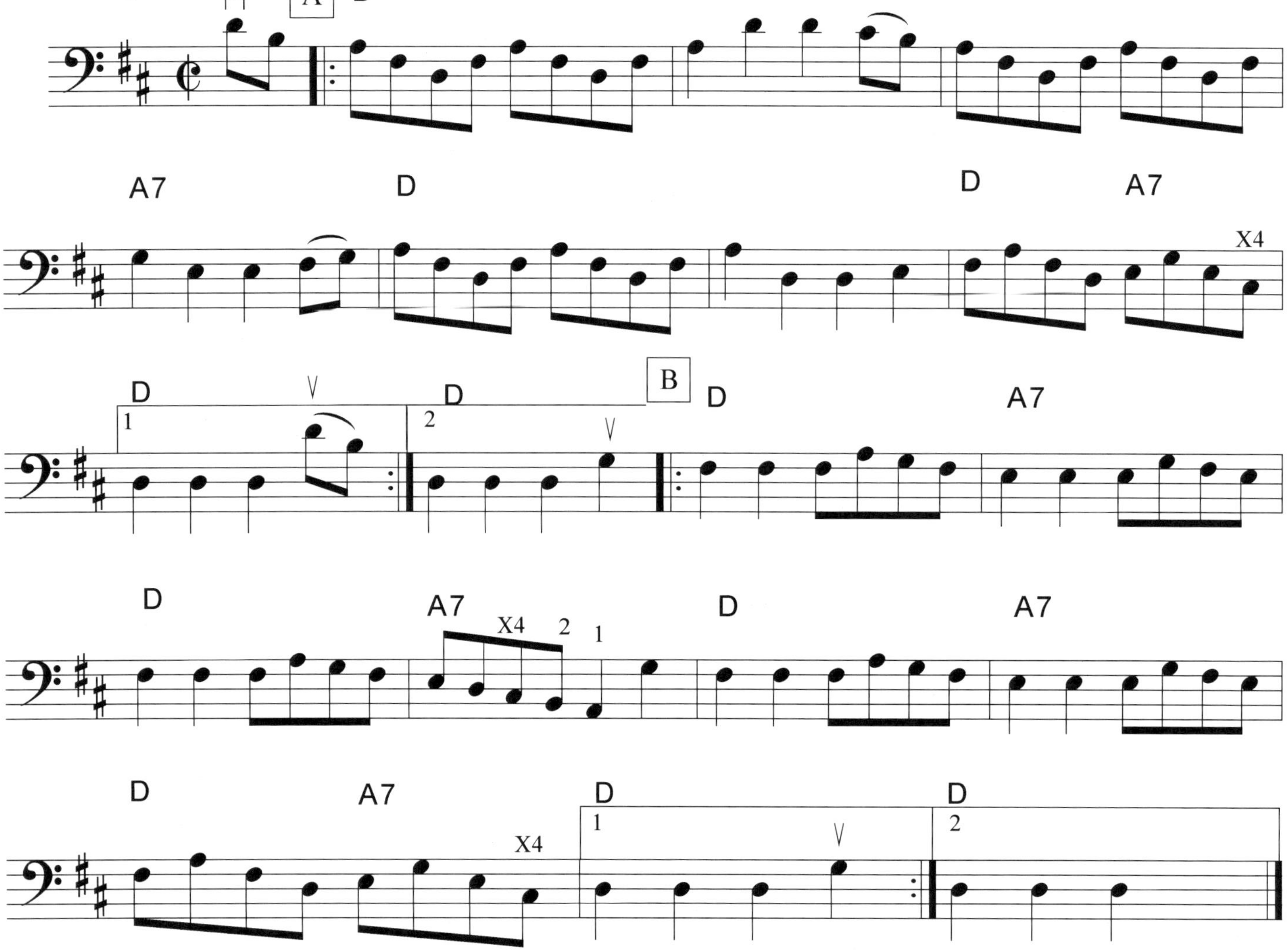

These variations can be used in place of the B section in "Soldier's Joy" to add variety. An example of using the variations can be heard on the audio track.

Variation 1

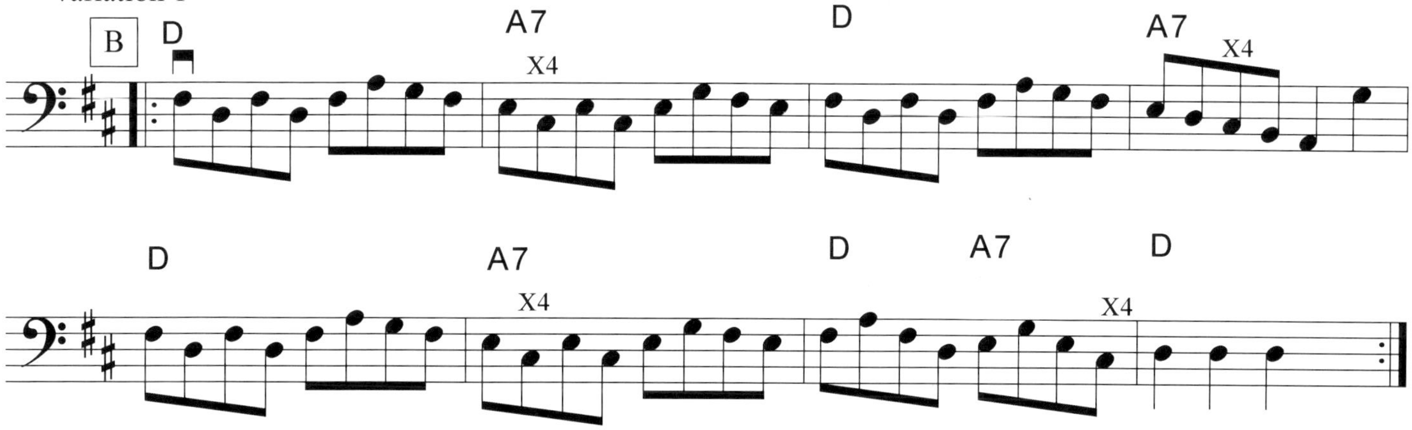


Variation 2

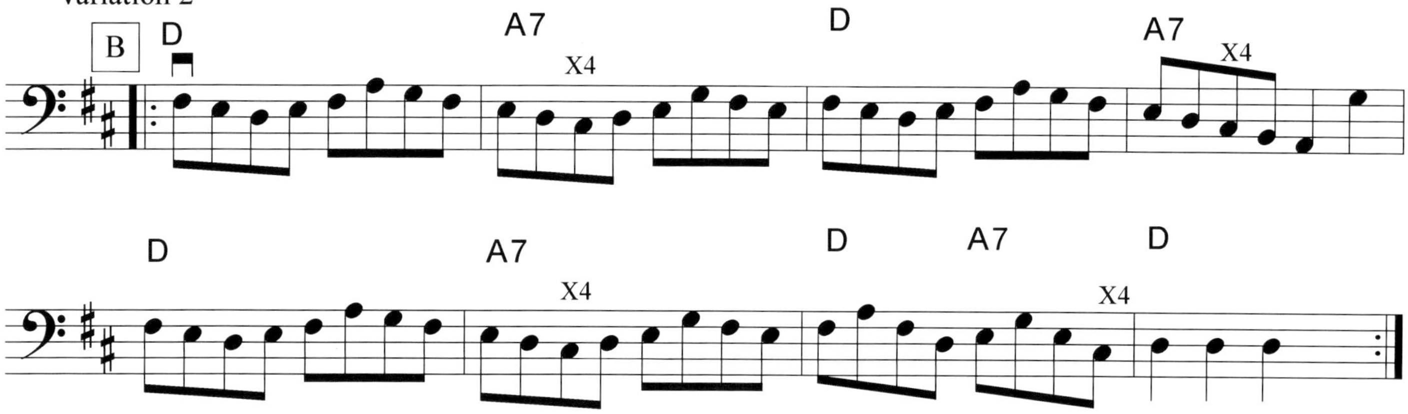

# Arkansas Traveler

"Arkansas Traveler" is a reel with a familiar melody.

Straight rhythm
Fast tempo

Traditional

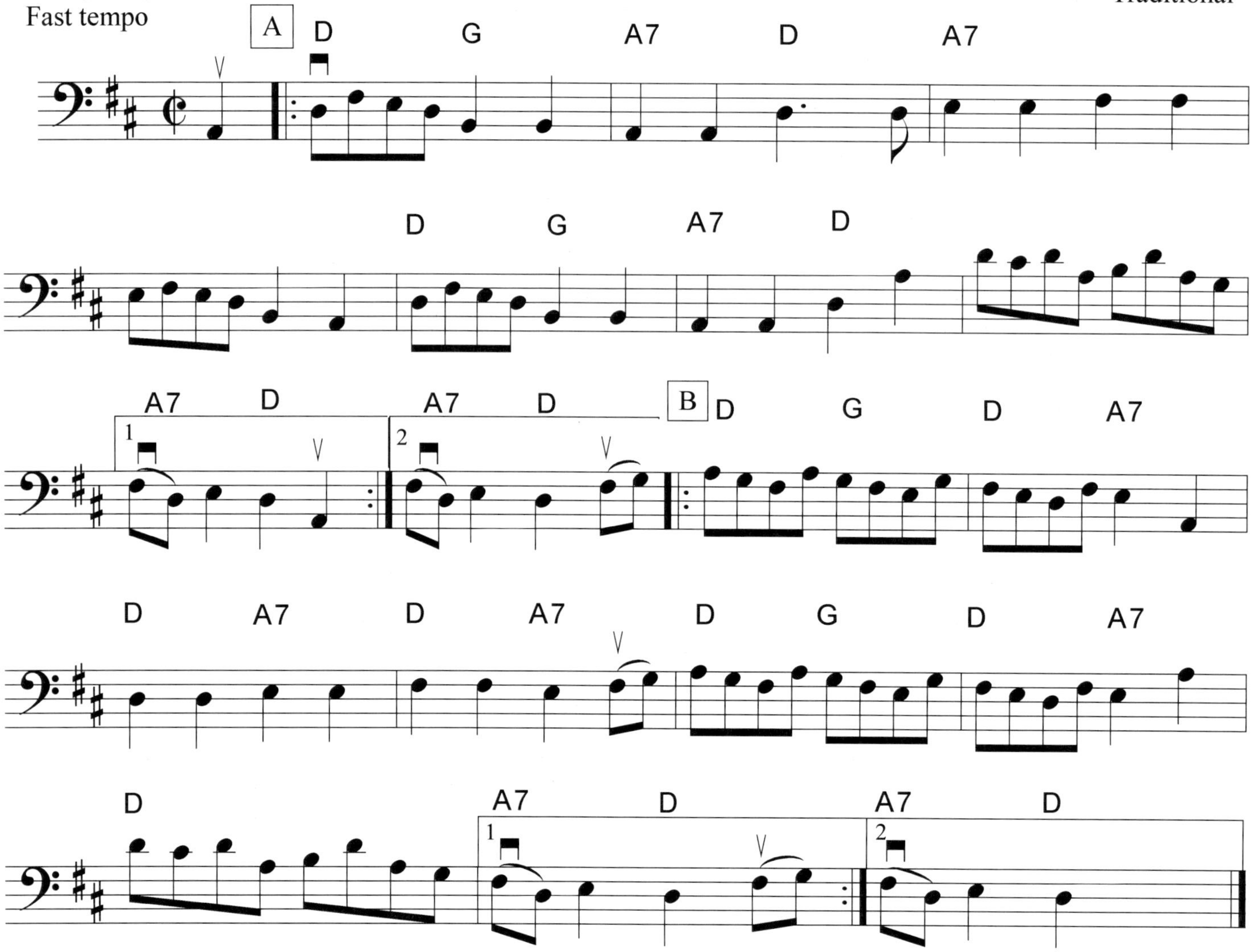

Part A of this tune can be played an octave higher as follows:

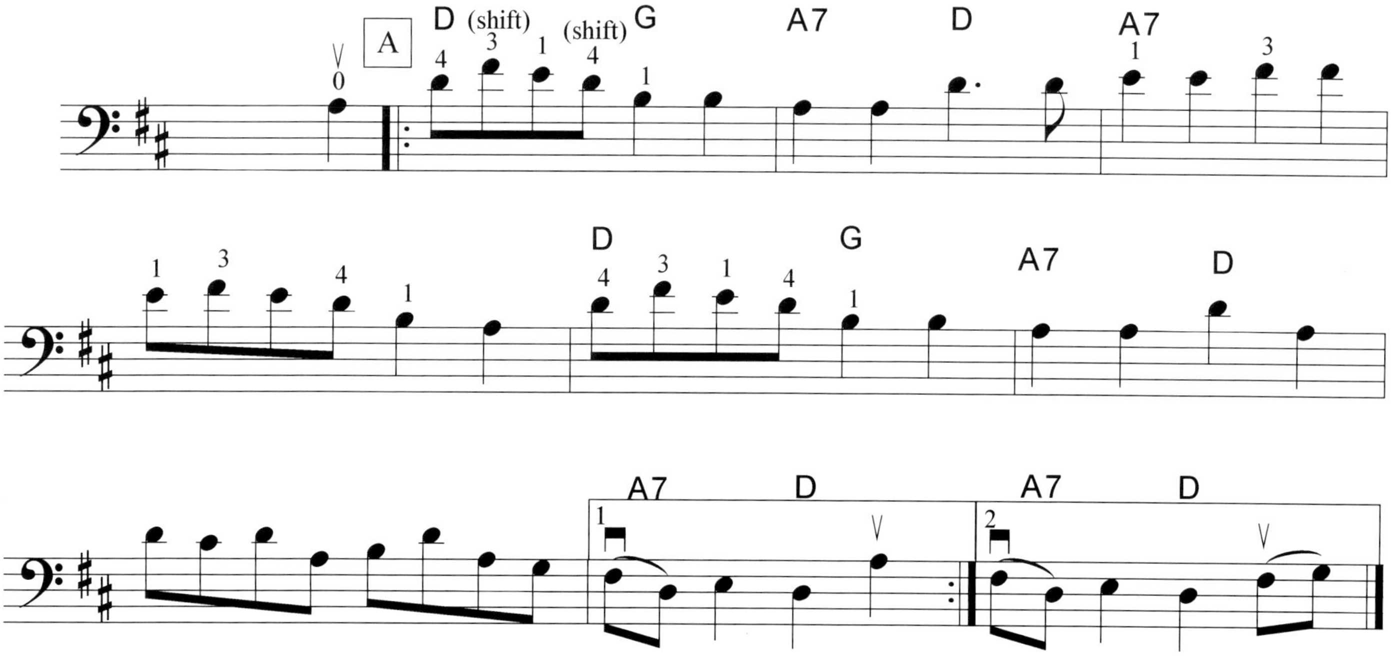

# Devil's Dream

"Devil's Dream" is traditionally played in the key of A but it can easily be played in the key of D as well. Two fingering options are marked in the A part.

Straight rhythm
Fast tempo

Traditional

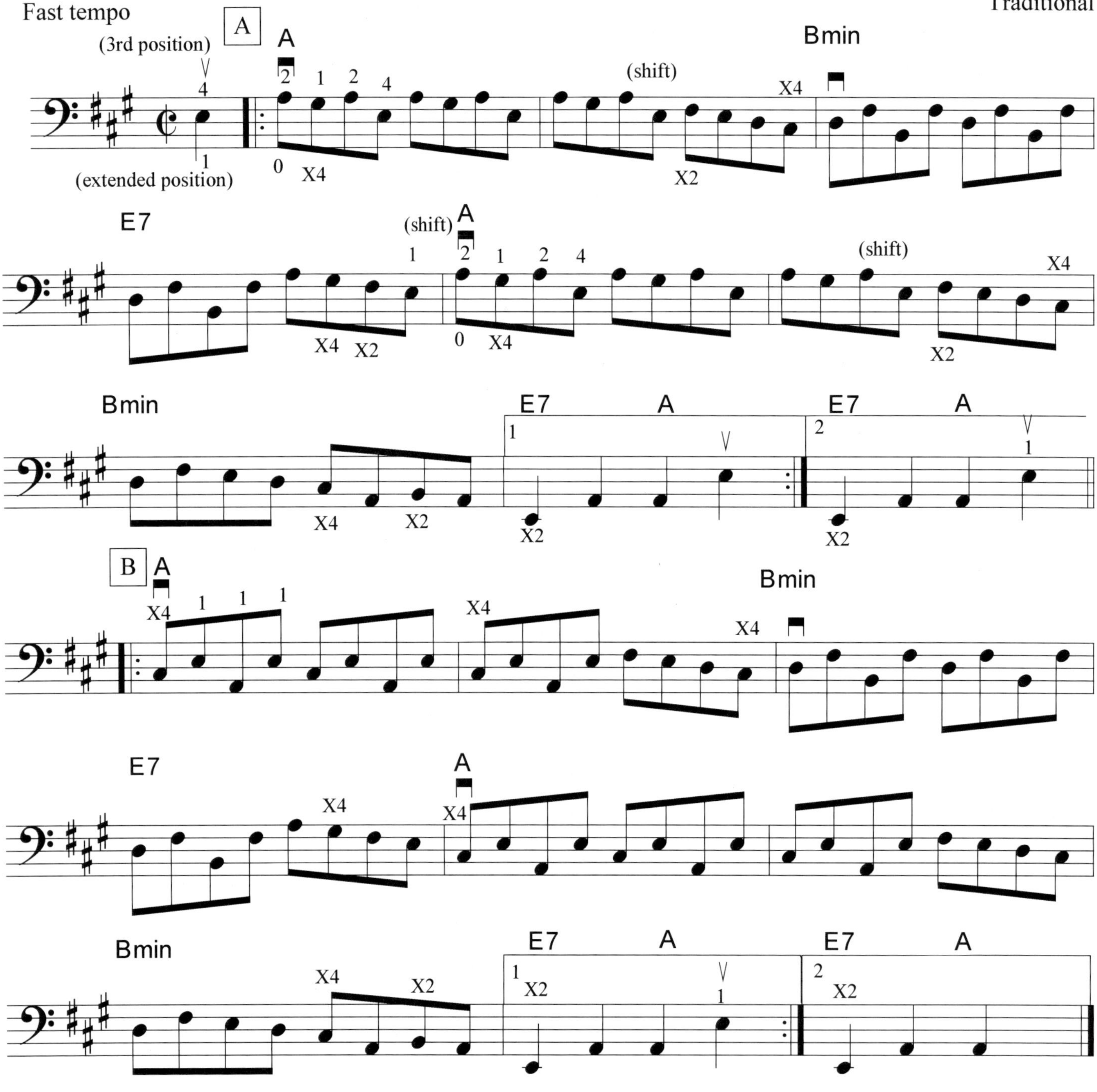

# Devil's Dream

This version can be played in a medley with other tunes in the key of D.

Straight rhythm
Fast tempo

Traditional

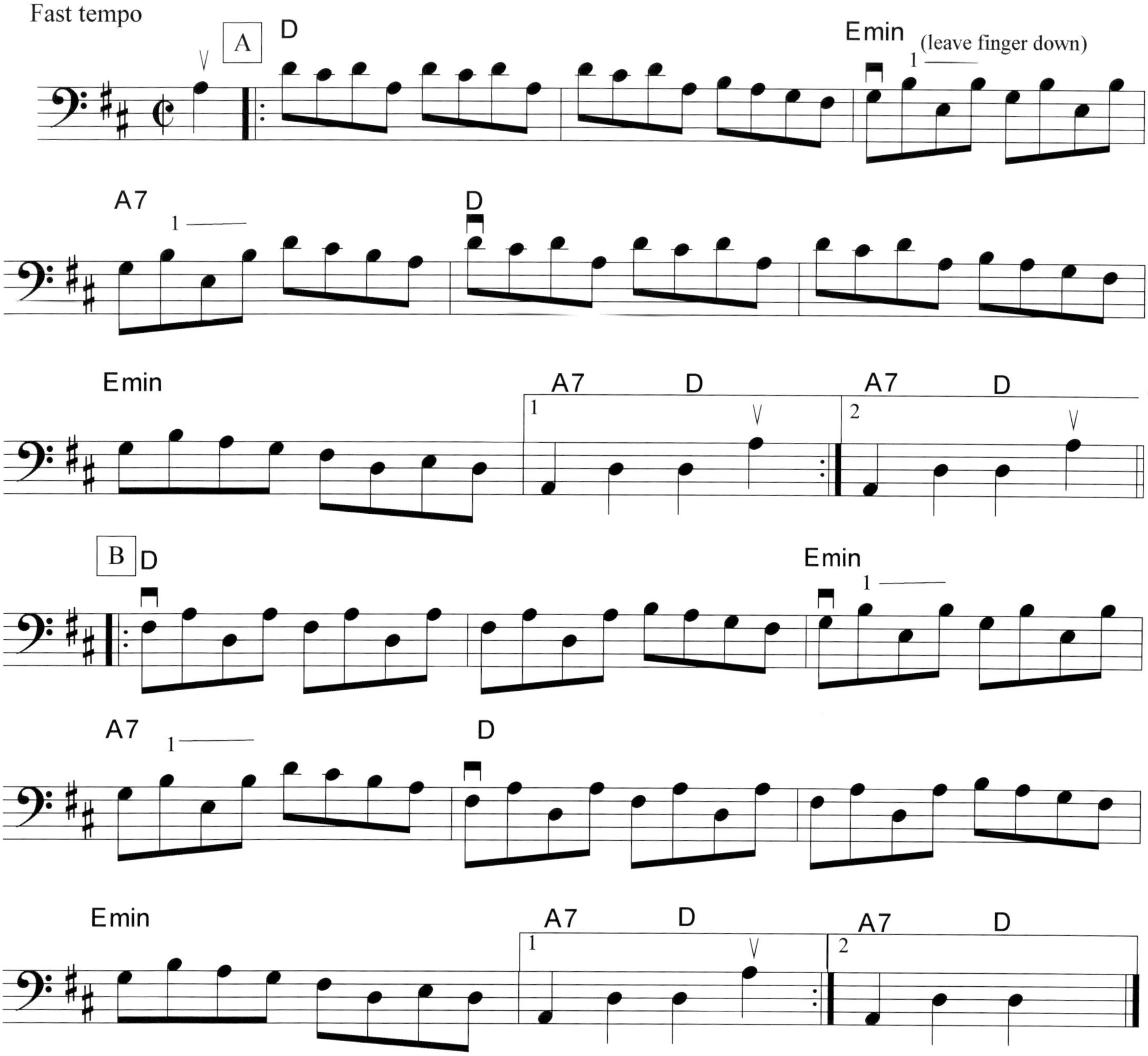

# Staten Island

(Simplified)

This version has been modified to simplify the fingering.

Swing rhythm
Moderate tempo

Traditional

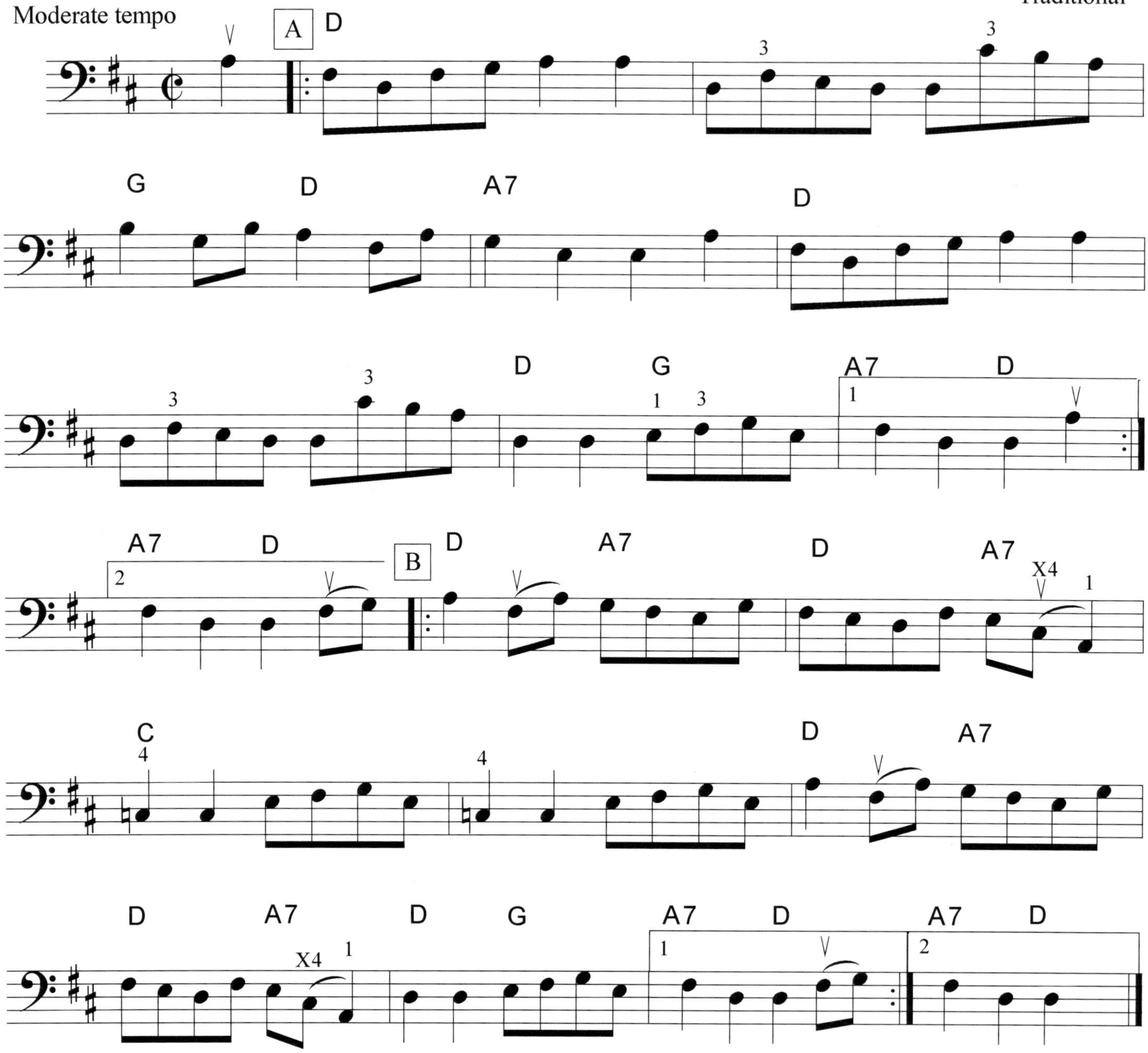

# Staten Island

(Lower, original version)

In "Staten Island" you can use a more swingy rhythm on the eighth-note passages. This rhythm will give the tune a different feel than playing straight eighth notes.

Swing rhythm
Moderate tempo

Traditional

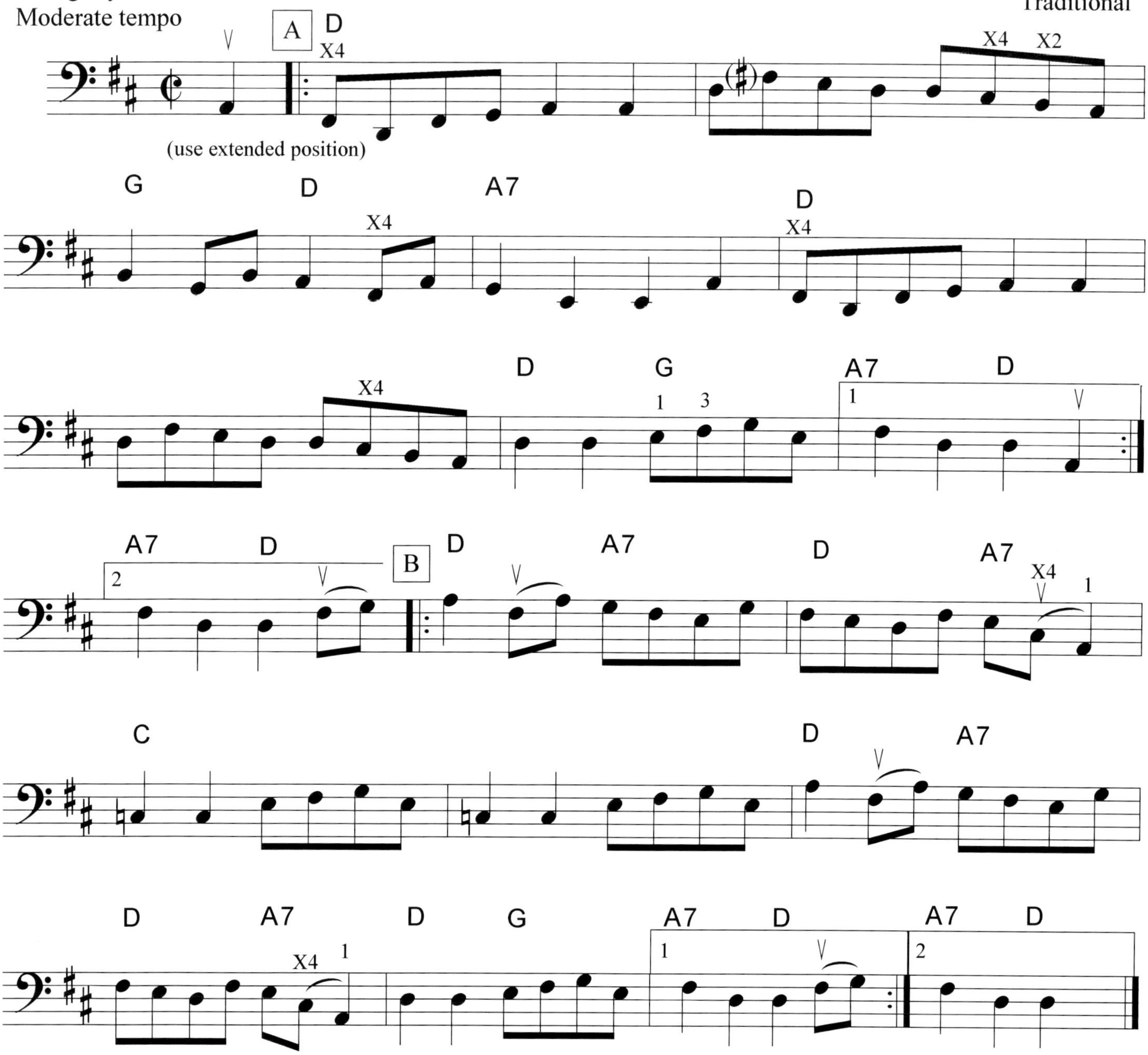

# Irish Washerwoman

Straight rhythm
Fast tempo

Traditional
Irish Jig

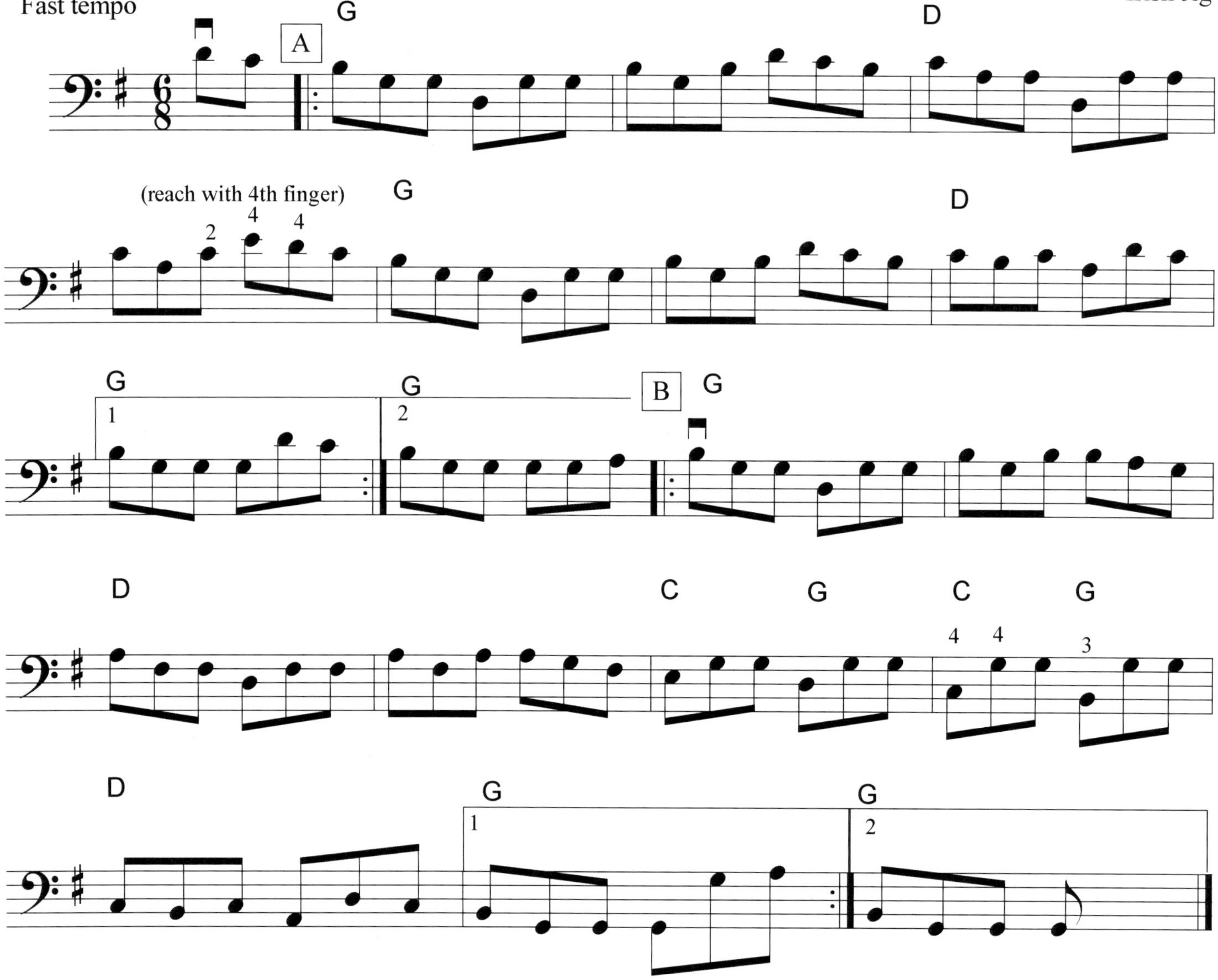

# Garry Owen

This traditional tune could be played in a medley with "Irish Washerwoman". Slurs have been added for smoothness, but the song could be played without slurs. "Garry Owen" is said to have been one of the songs played by a band as the 7th Cavalry headed out towards Little Big Horn. It was Custer's favorite battle tune.

Straight rhythm
Fast tempo

Traditional

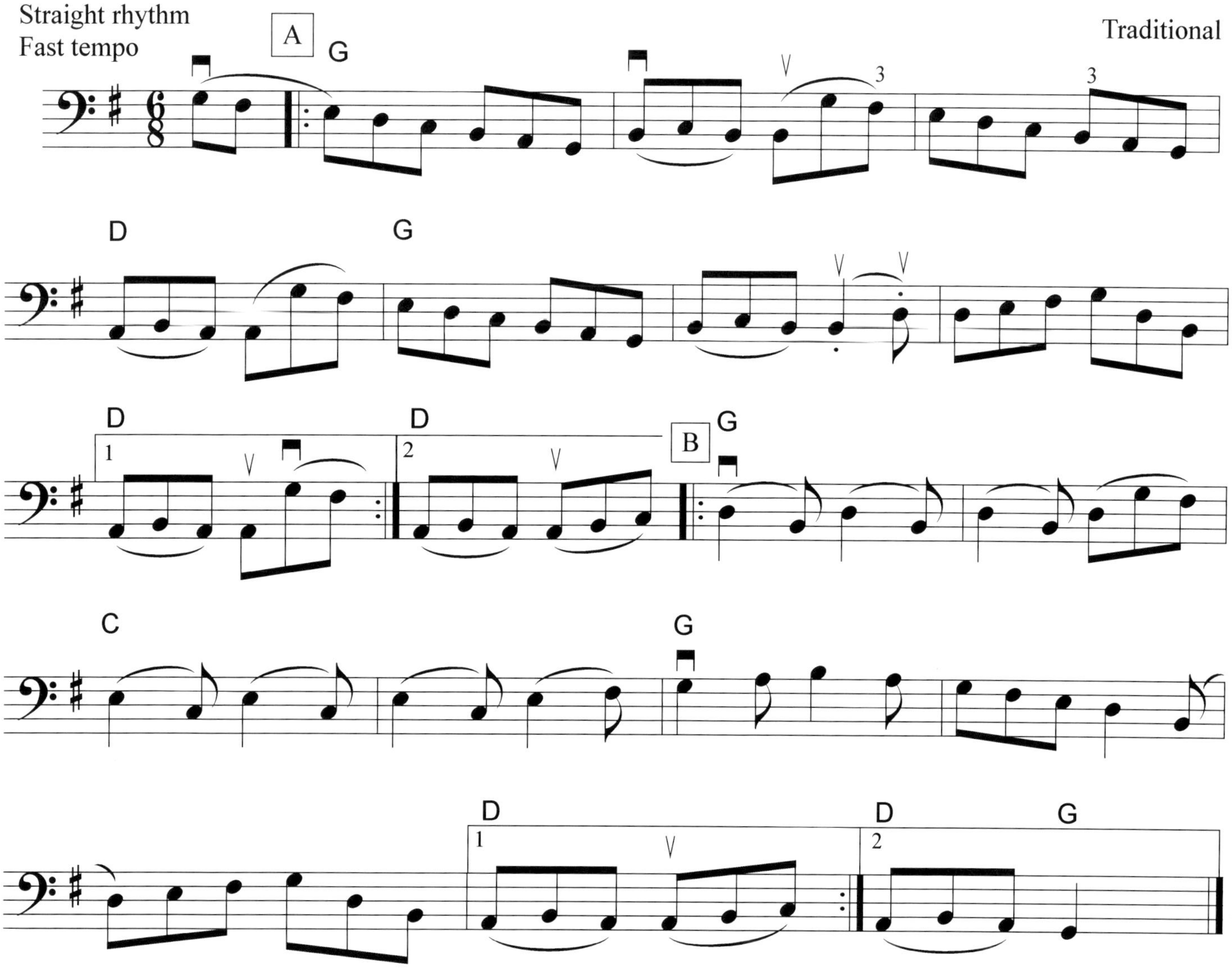

10

# Red Haired Boy

(Simplified)

This version has been modified to simplify the fingering.

Straight or swing rhythm
Moderate tempo

Traditional

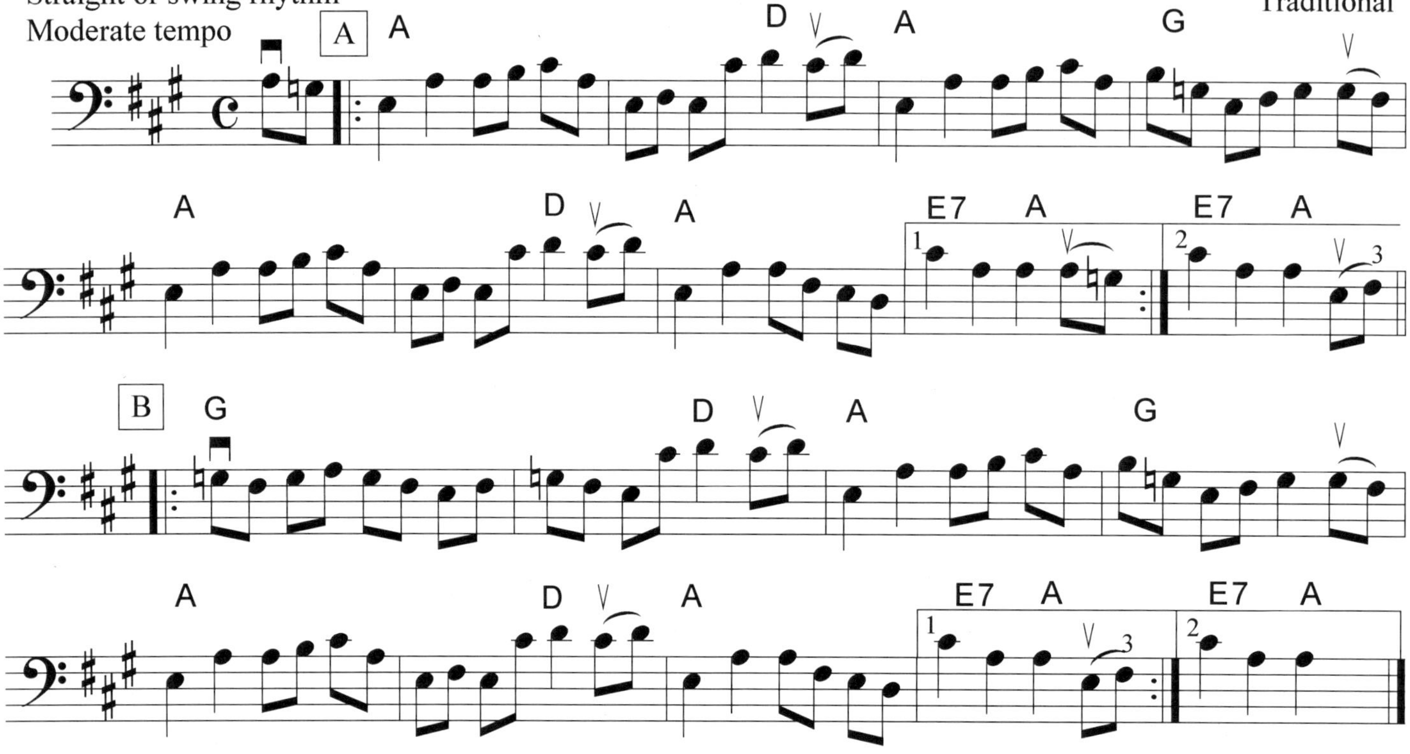


11

# Red Haired Boy

(Lower, original version)

Straight or swing rhythm

Traditional

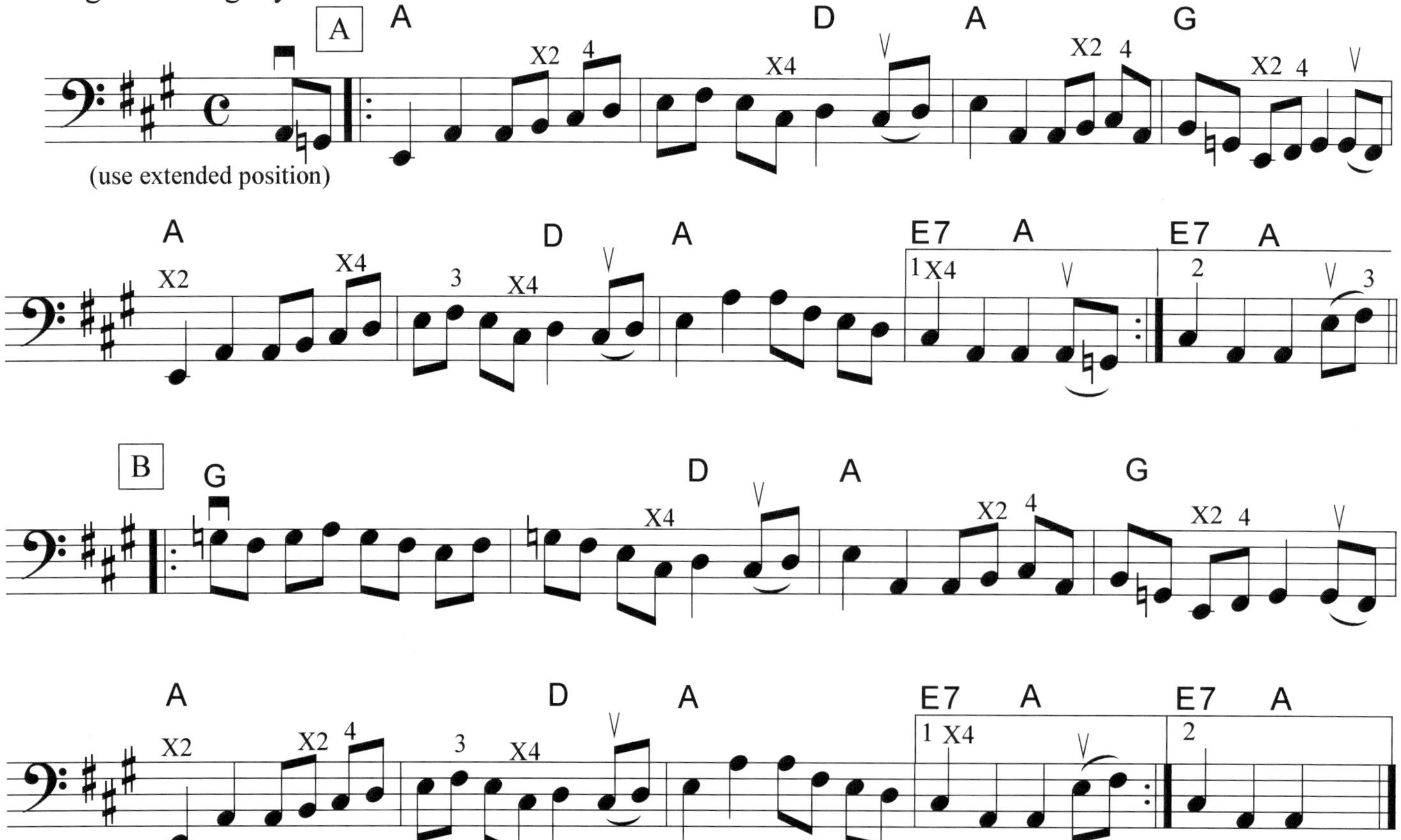

12

# Red Haired Boy

(Variation)

Straight or swing rhythm
Moderate tempo

Traditional

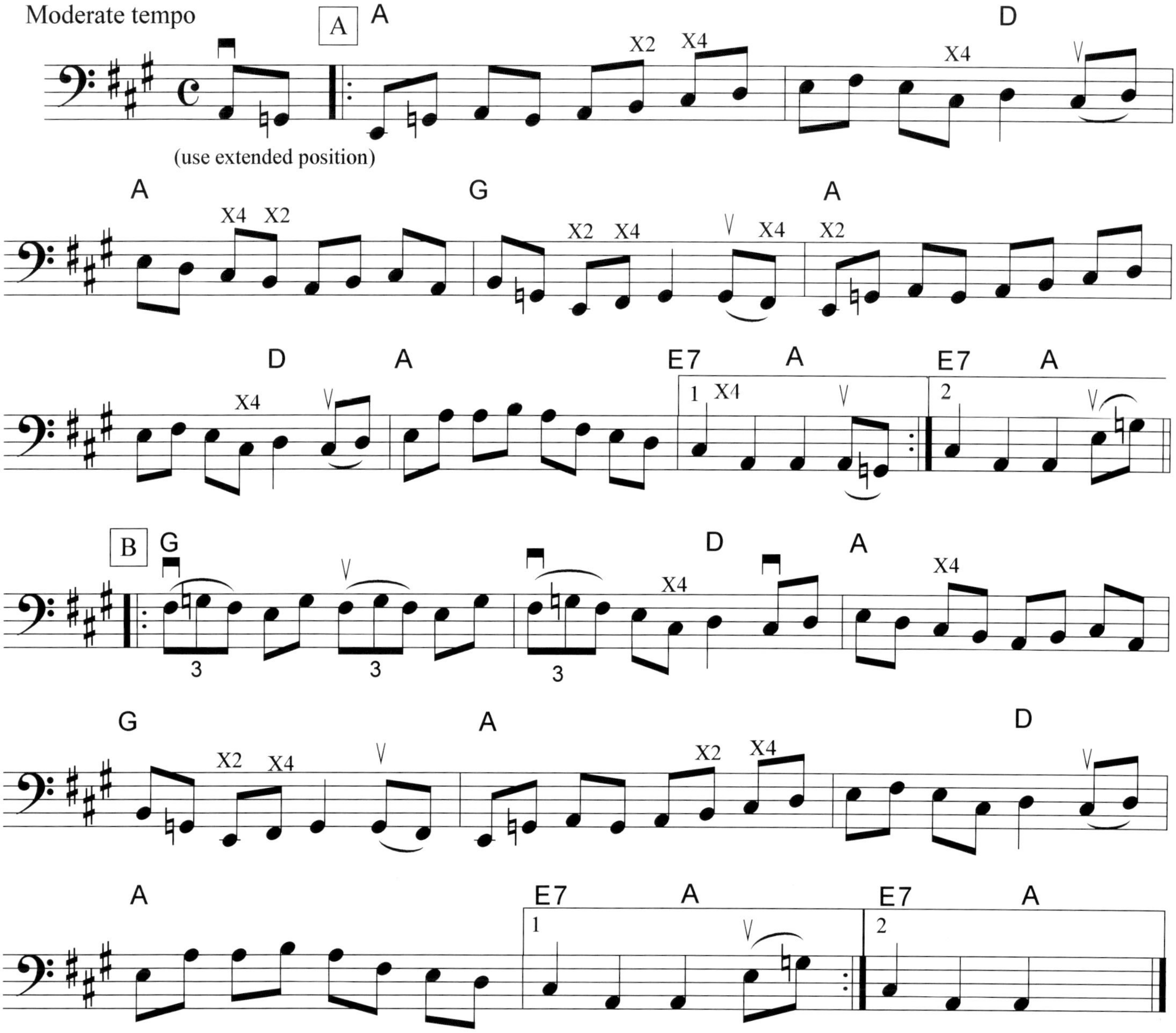


In old-time fiddling each player has their own unique style, and you can hear different fiddlers play the same song with many variations. Improvisation is an important part of the development of different styles. "Red Haired Boy"can be used as an example of how to change passages with simple improvisation. To give the tune a more swingy feel, use a swing rhythm on all eighth-note passages.

Both versions of "Red Haired Boy" could be played one after the other. This would add variety and interest to the song if you are playing it through more than once.

13

# Wilson's Clog

(Simplified)

This version has been modified to simplify the fingering.
It is written here in 6/8 time to make the rhythm easier to read.

Traditional

Fast or moderate tempo

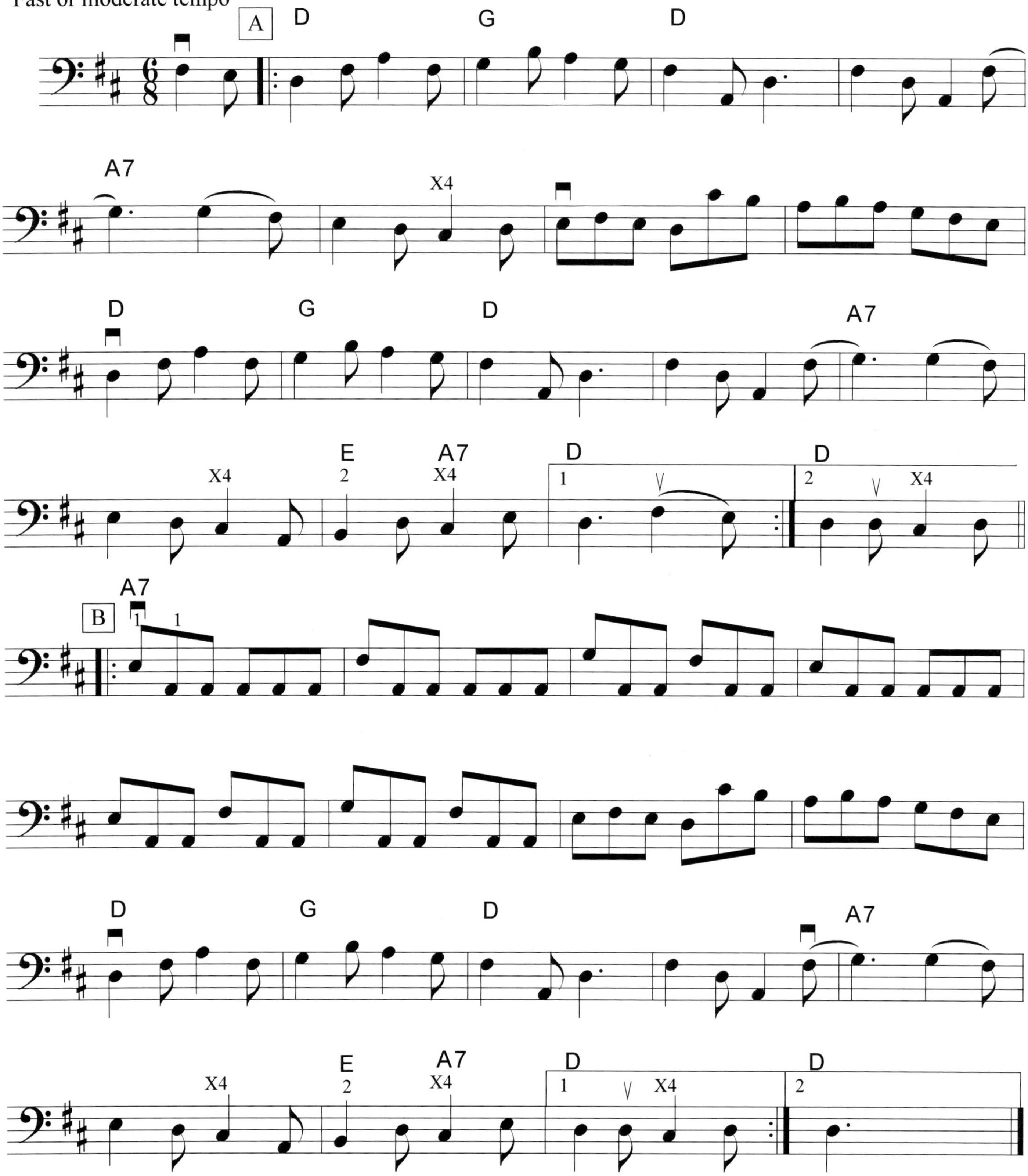

14

# Wilson's Clog

(Lower, original version)

"Wilson's Clog" is also known as "Fred Wilson's Clog" or "Fred Wilson's Hornpipe". It is written here in 6/8 time to make the rhythm easier to read.

Fast or moderate tempo

Traditional

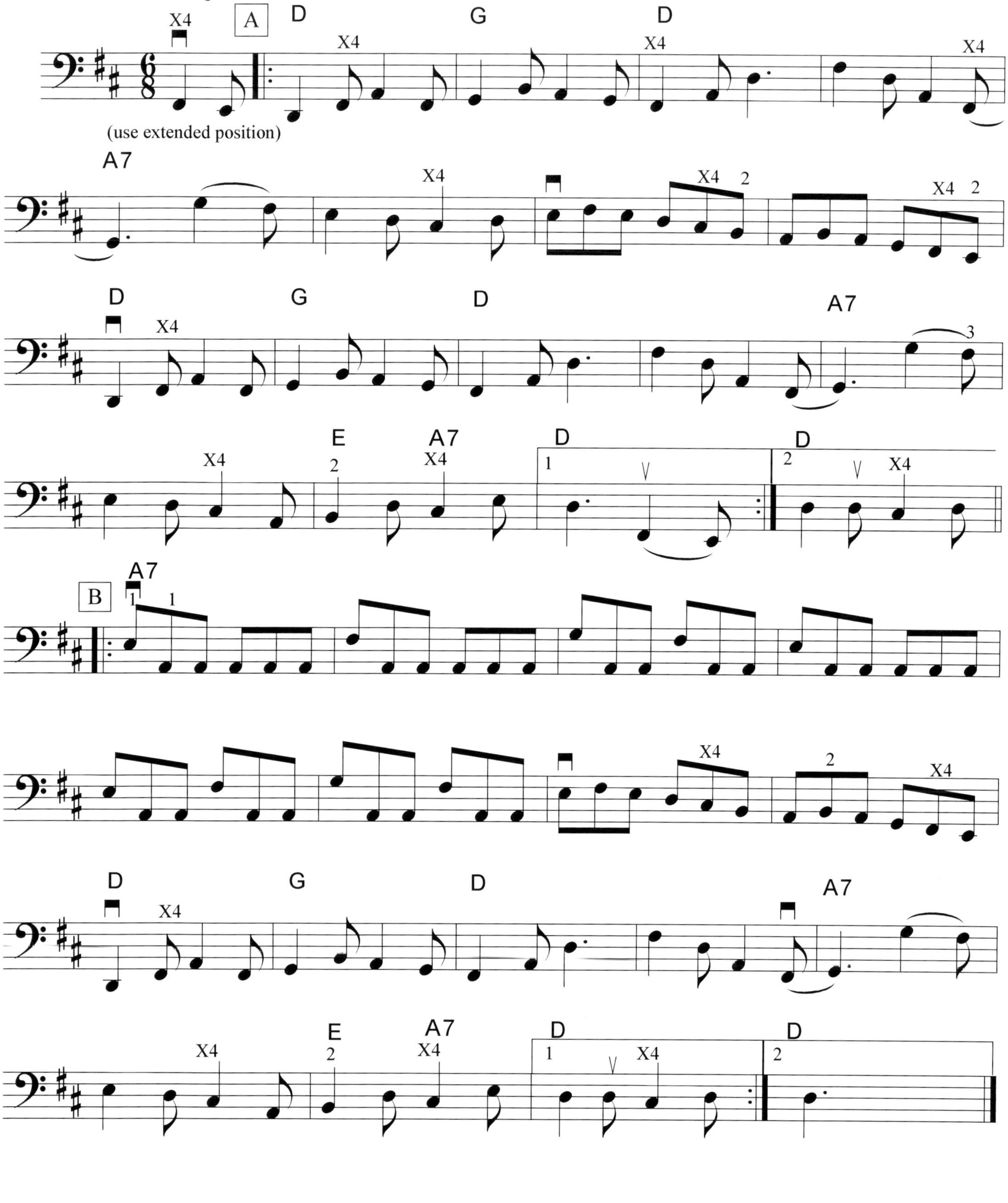

15

# Here's to the Ladies

(Simplified)

This version has been modified to simplify the fingering.

Straight rhythm
Fast tempo

Traditional

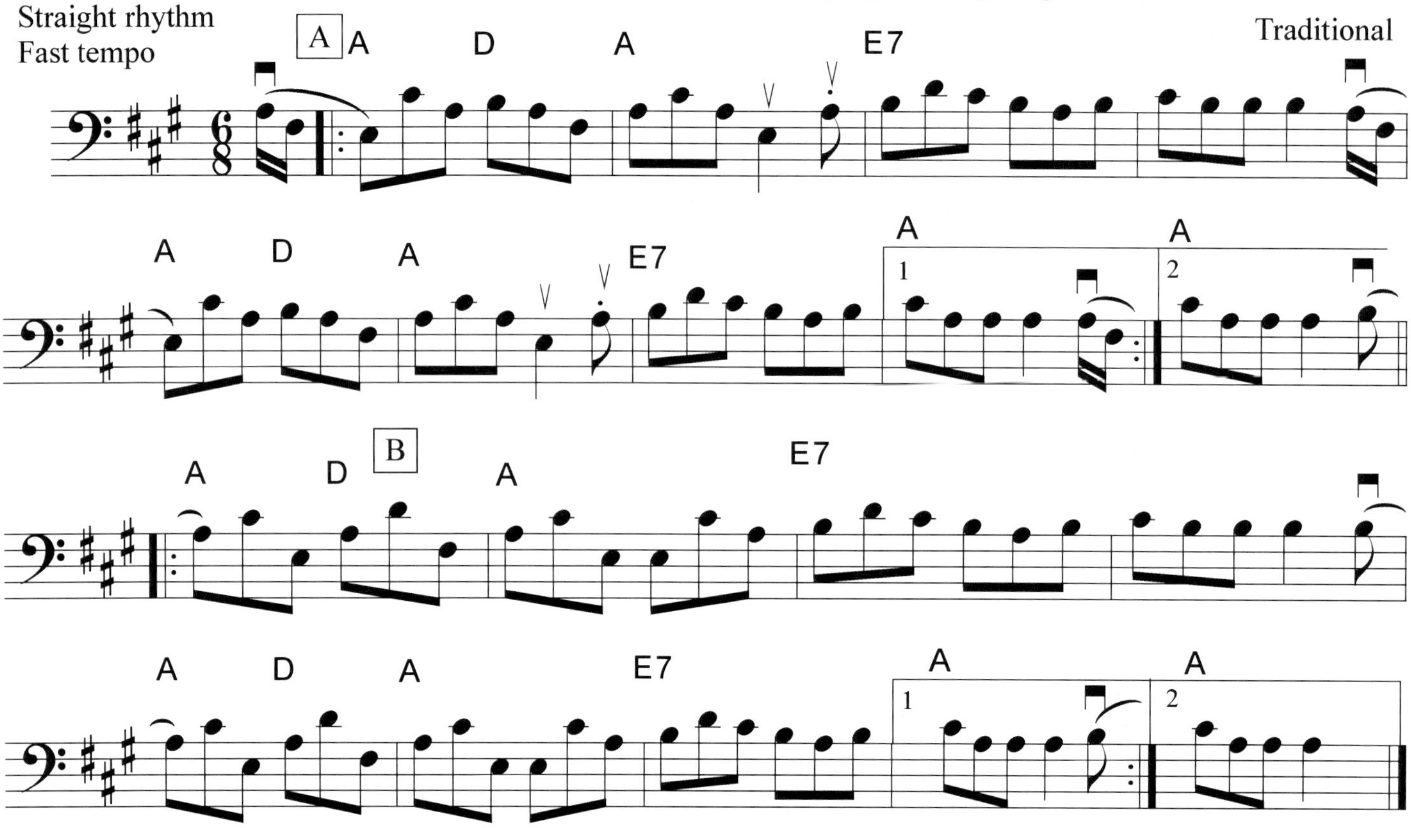


16

# Here's to the Ladies

(Lower, original version)

Straight rhythm
Fast tempo

Traditional

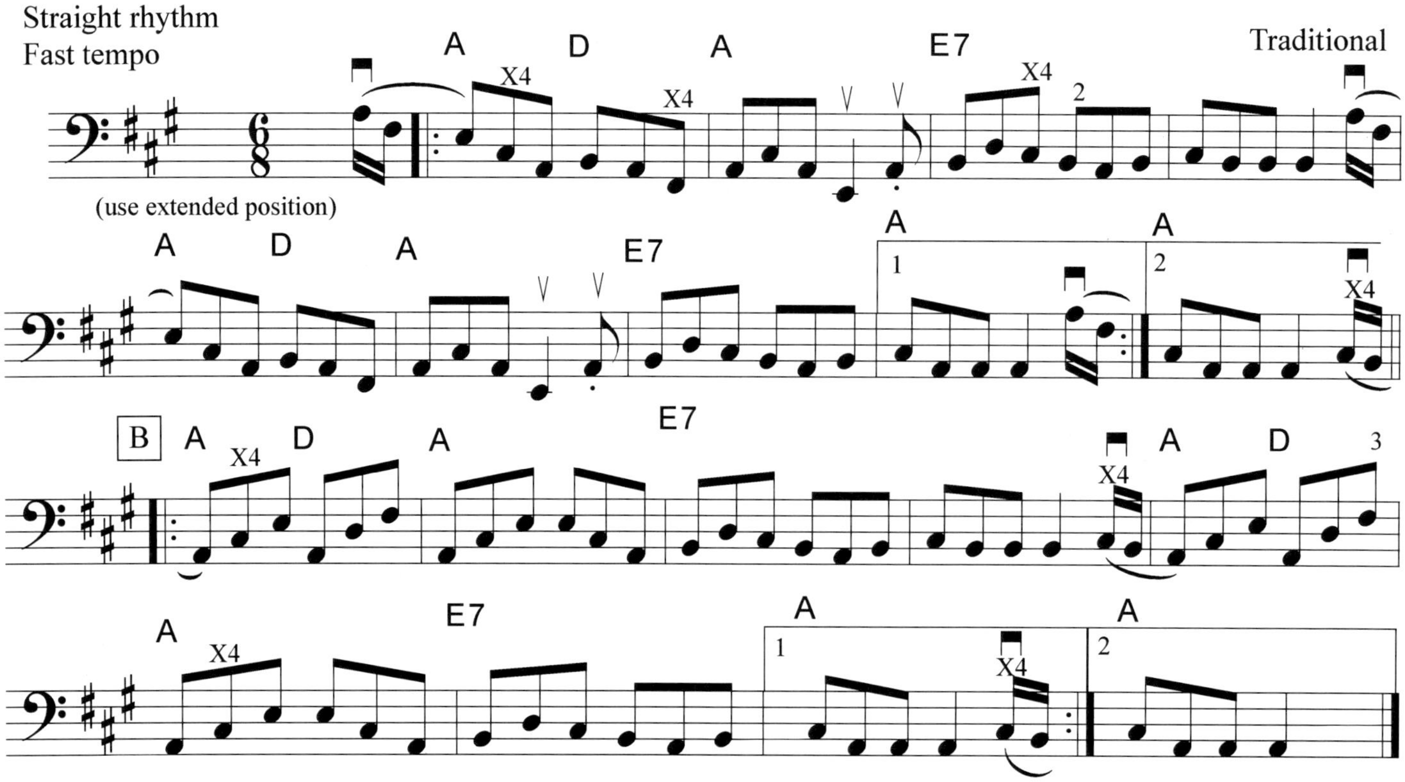

17

# St. Anne's Reel

(Simplified)

This version is modified to simplify the fingering.

Straight or swing rhythm
Fast or moderate tempo

Traditional

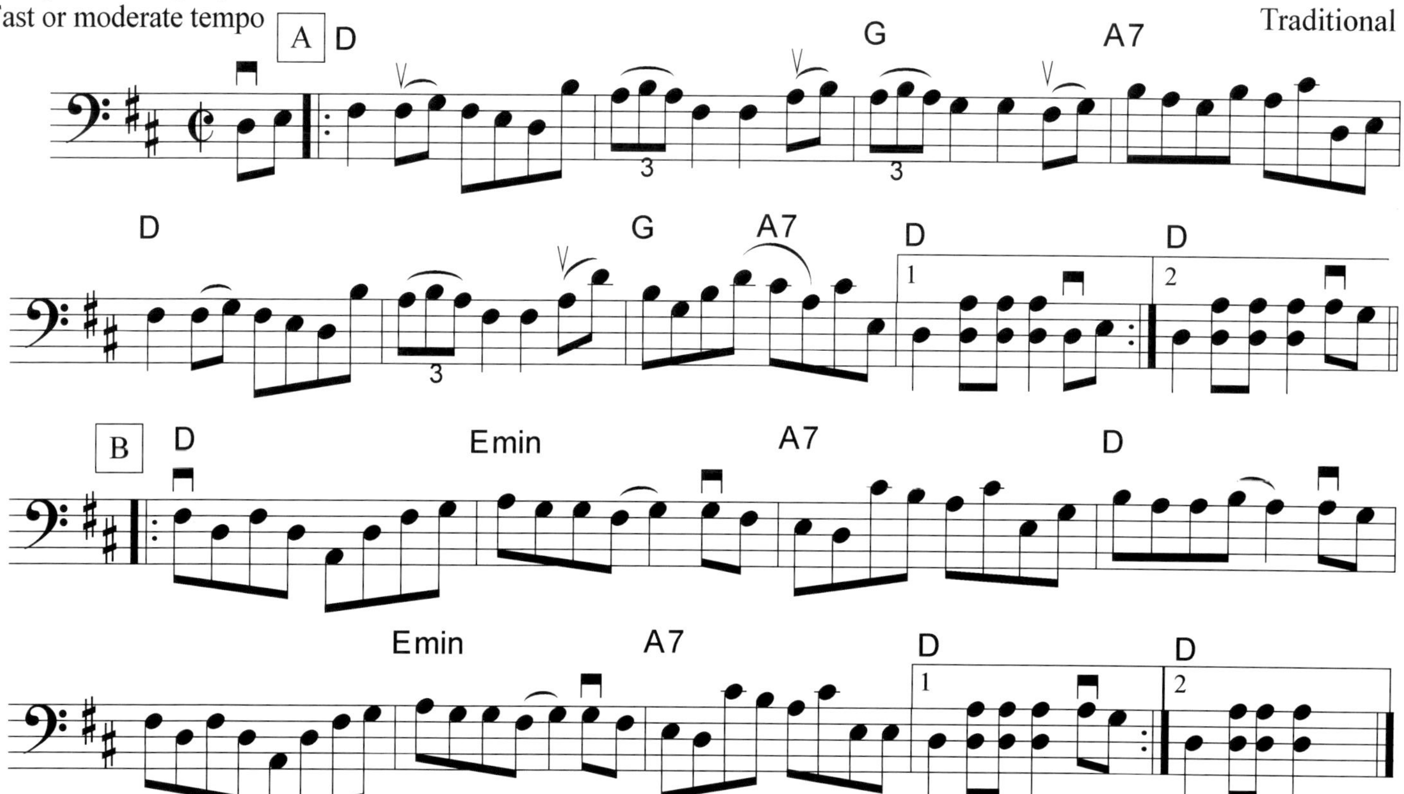


18

# St. Anne's Reel

(Lower, original version)

Straight or swing rhythm
Fast or moderate tempo

Traditional

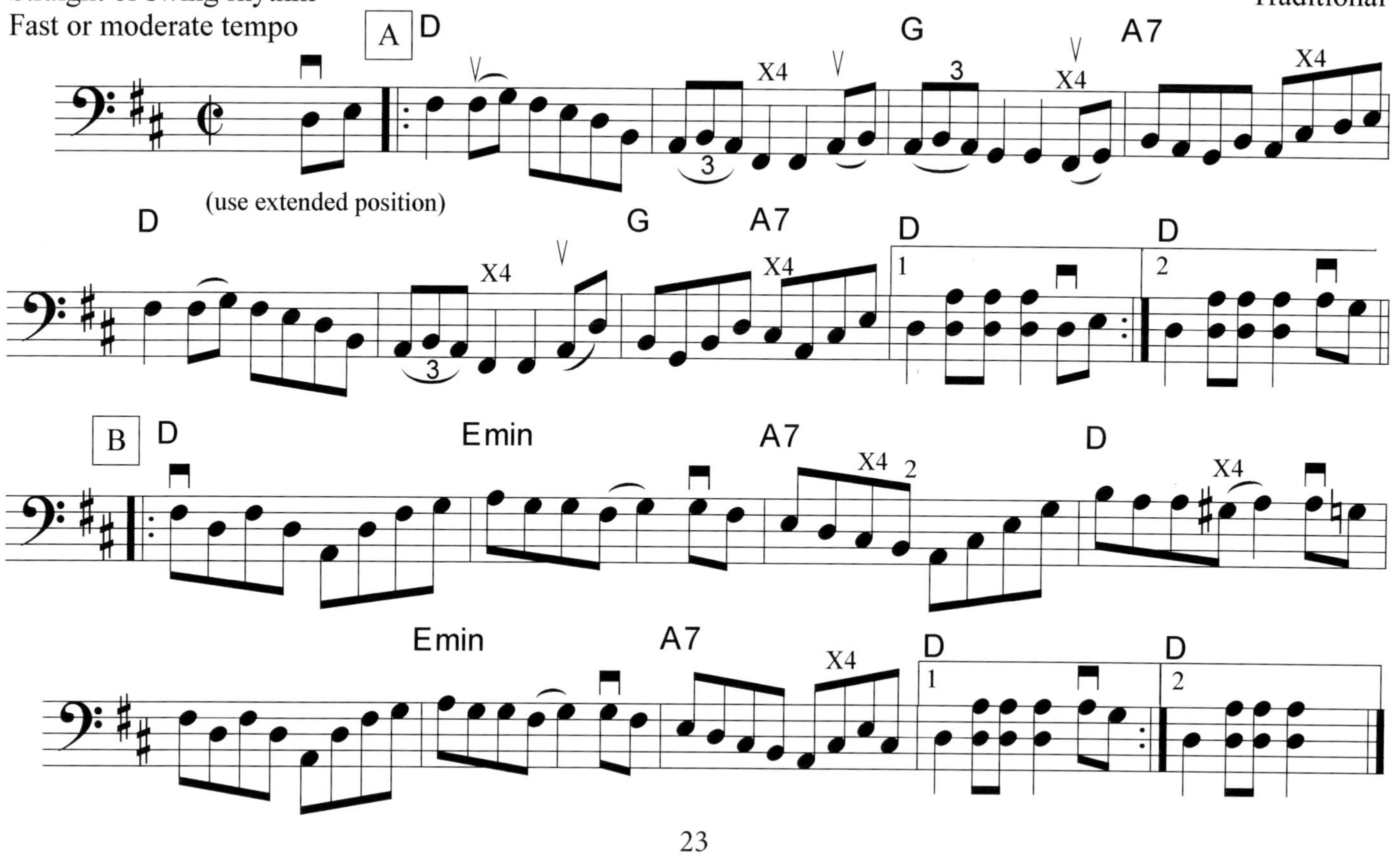

19

# Great Western Clog

This clog is also known as the "Great Western Lancashire Clog".
It has been written in 6/8 time to make the rhythm easier to read.

Moderate Tempo

Traditional

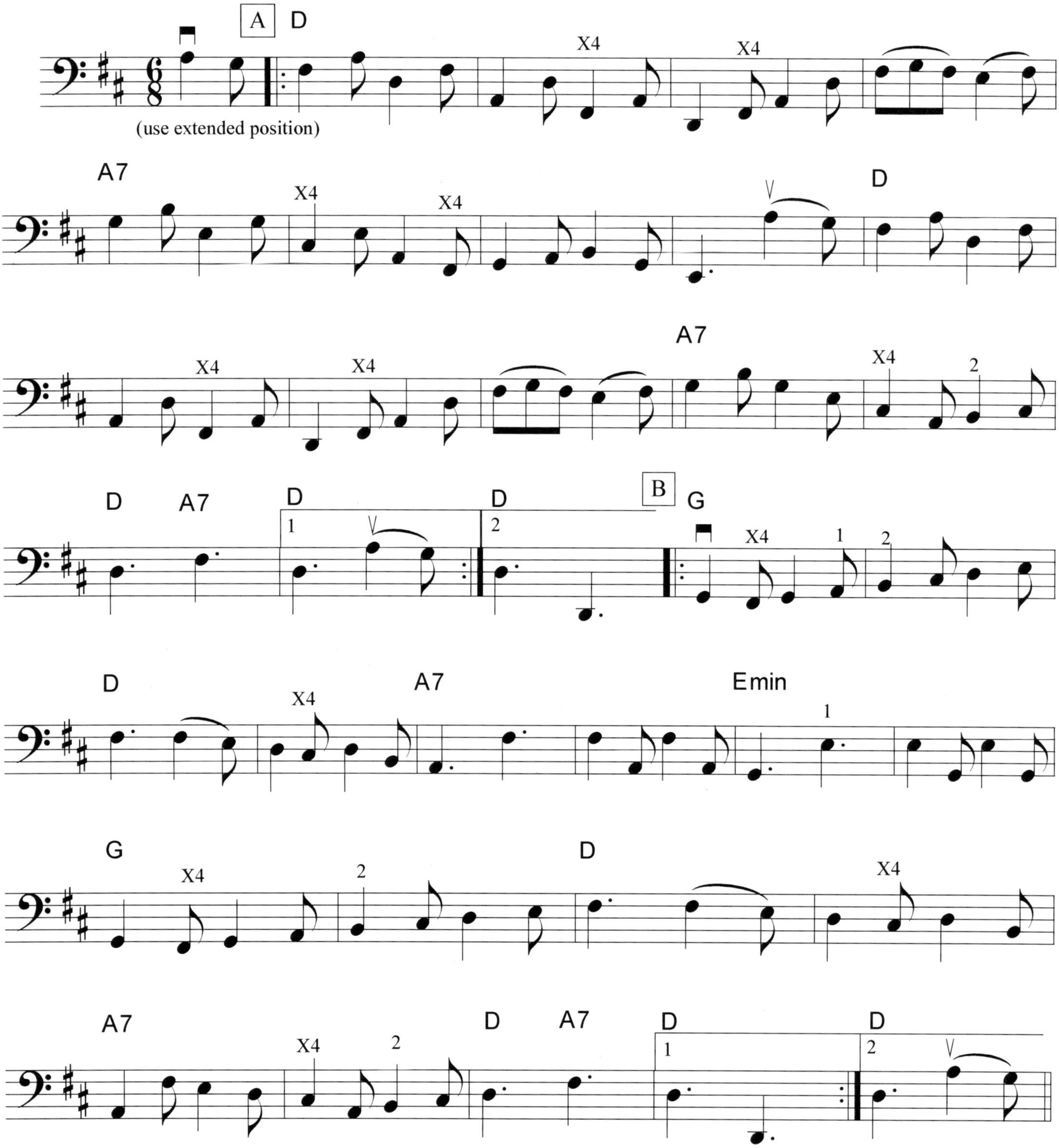

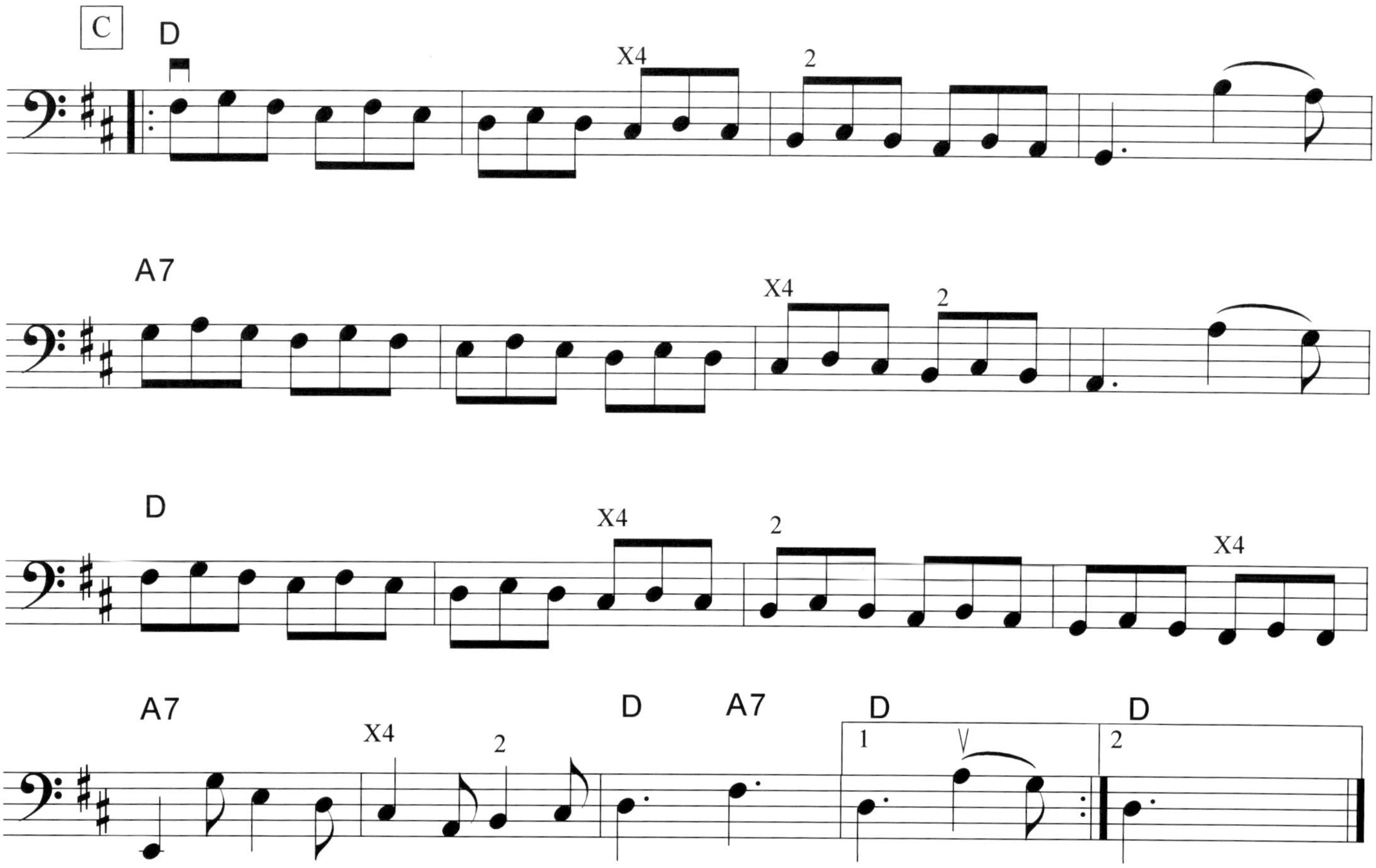
C
D
X4
2
A7
X4
2
D
X4
2
X4
A7
X4
2
D
A7
D
1
D
2

20

# East Tennessee Blues

Swing rhythm
Fast or moderate tempo

Old-time

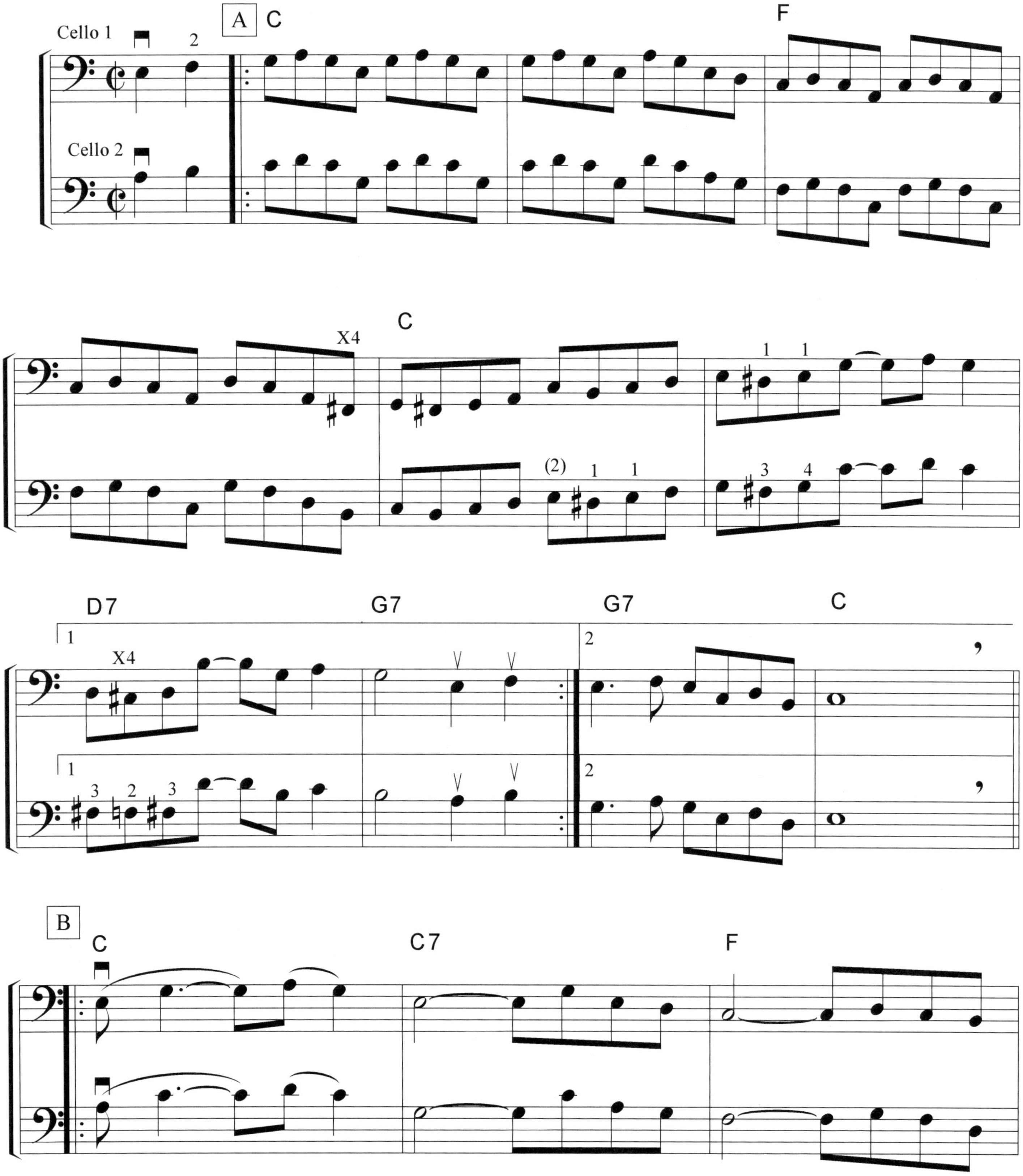

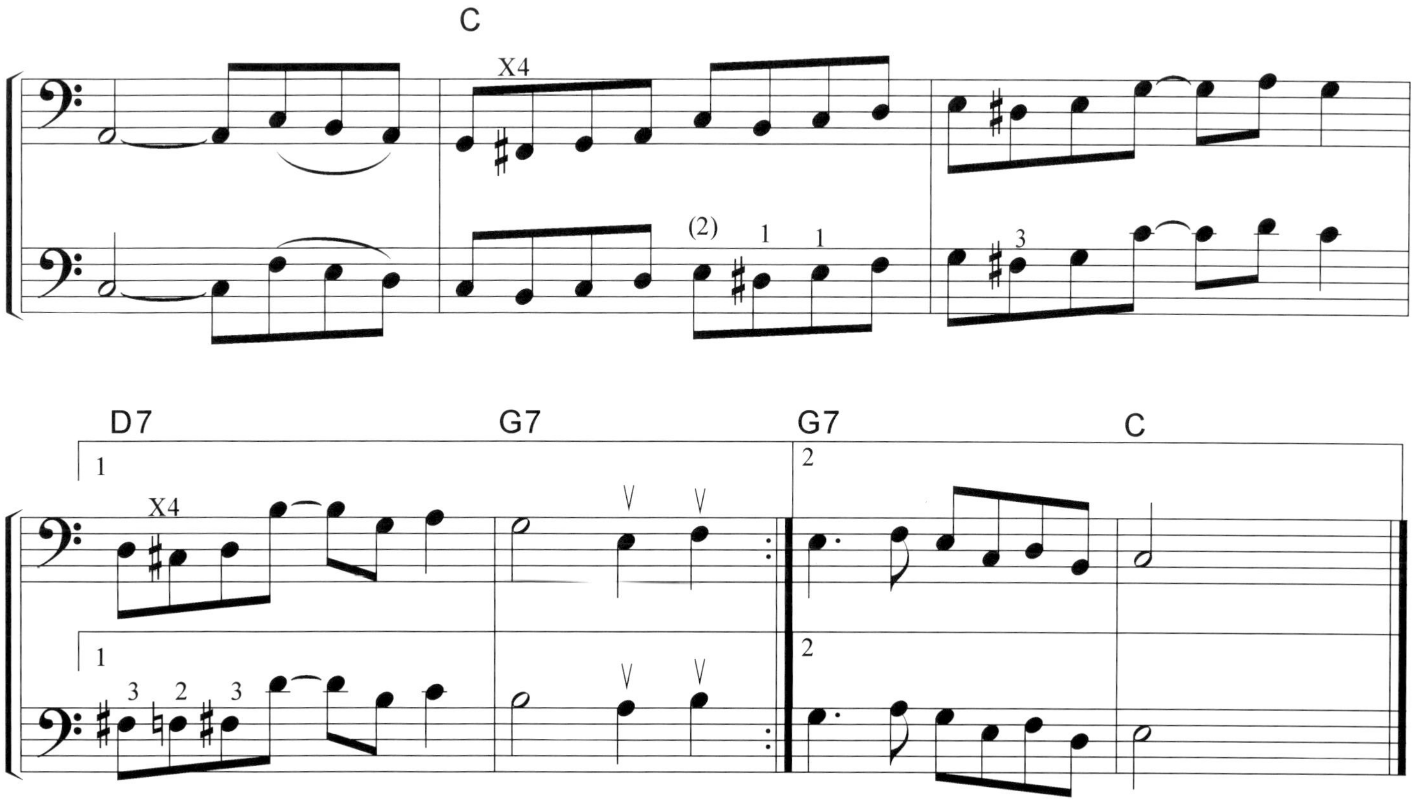
C
X4
(2) 1 1
3
D7
G7
G7
C
1
X4
2
1
3 2 3
2

21

# My Silver Bell

Swing rhythm
Fast or moderate tempo

Old-time

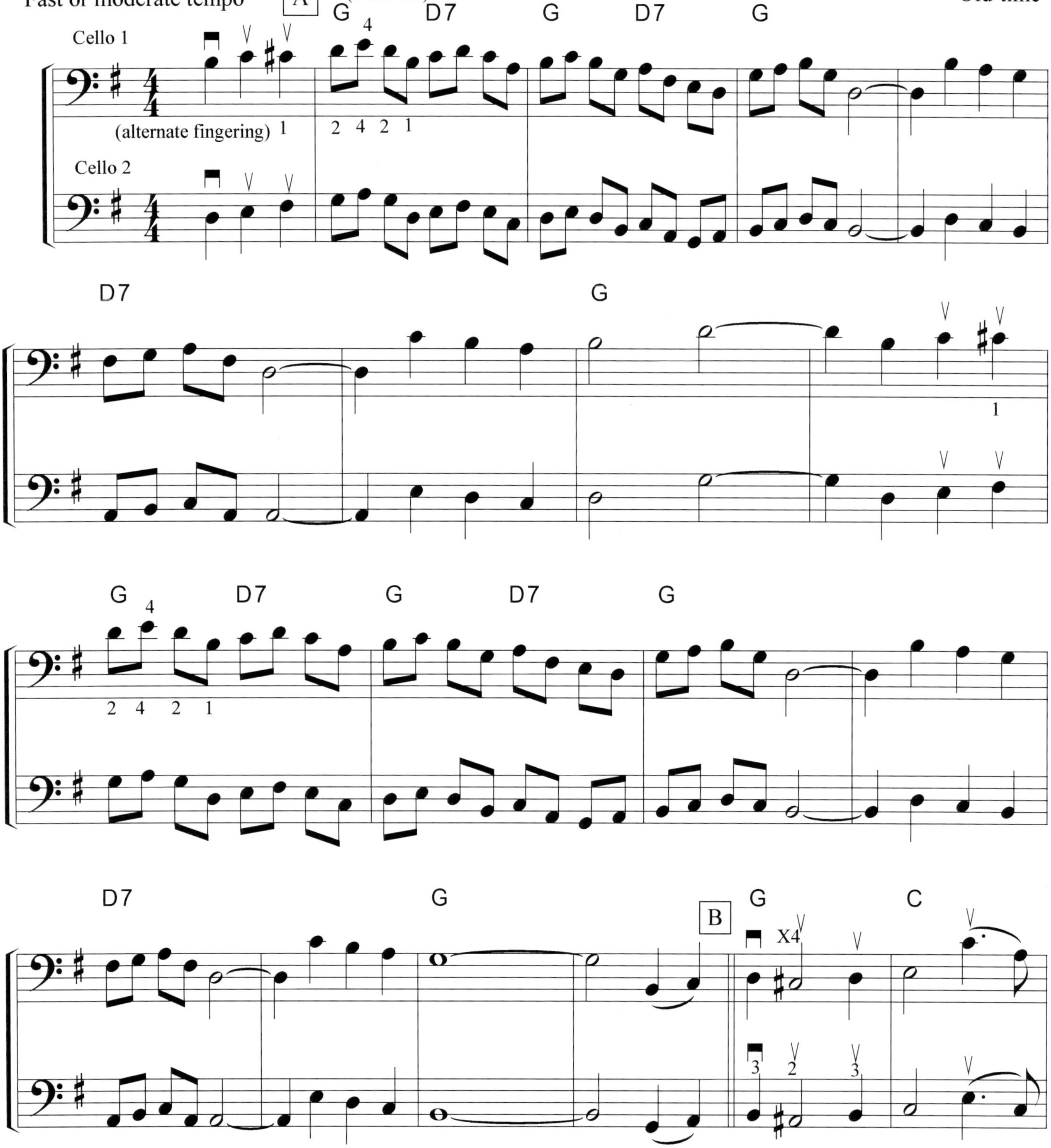

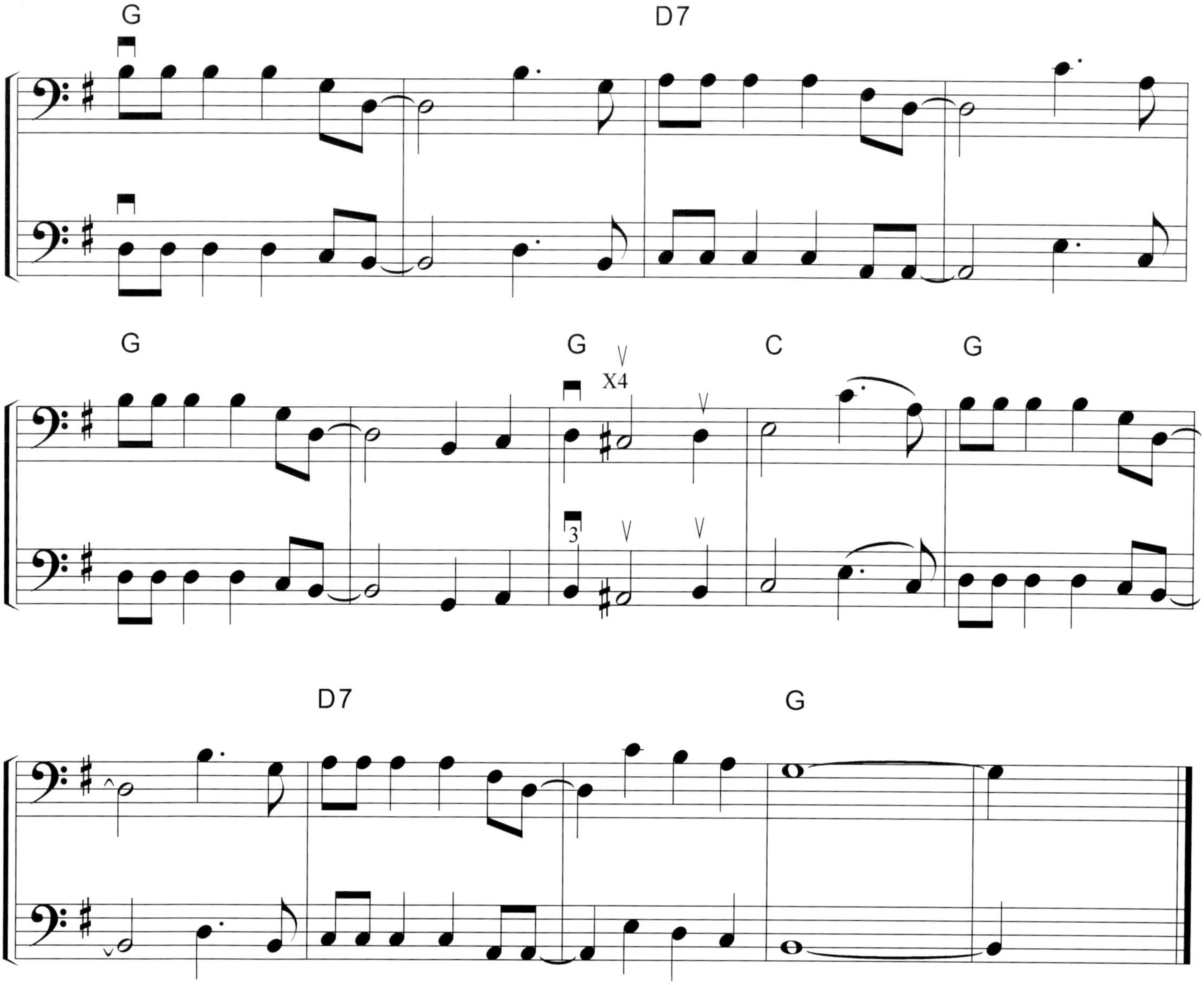
G
D7
G
G
X4
3
C
G
D7
G

22

# Whoa Mule

"Whoa Mule" uses finger slides to imitate the sound of a braying mule.
The symbol ⟋ means to slide your finger up to the note from one half step below.

Swing rhythm
Fast or moderate tempo

Attributed to
Tommy Jackson

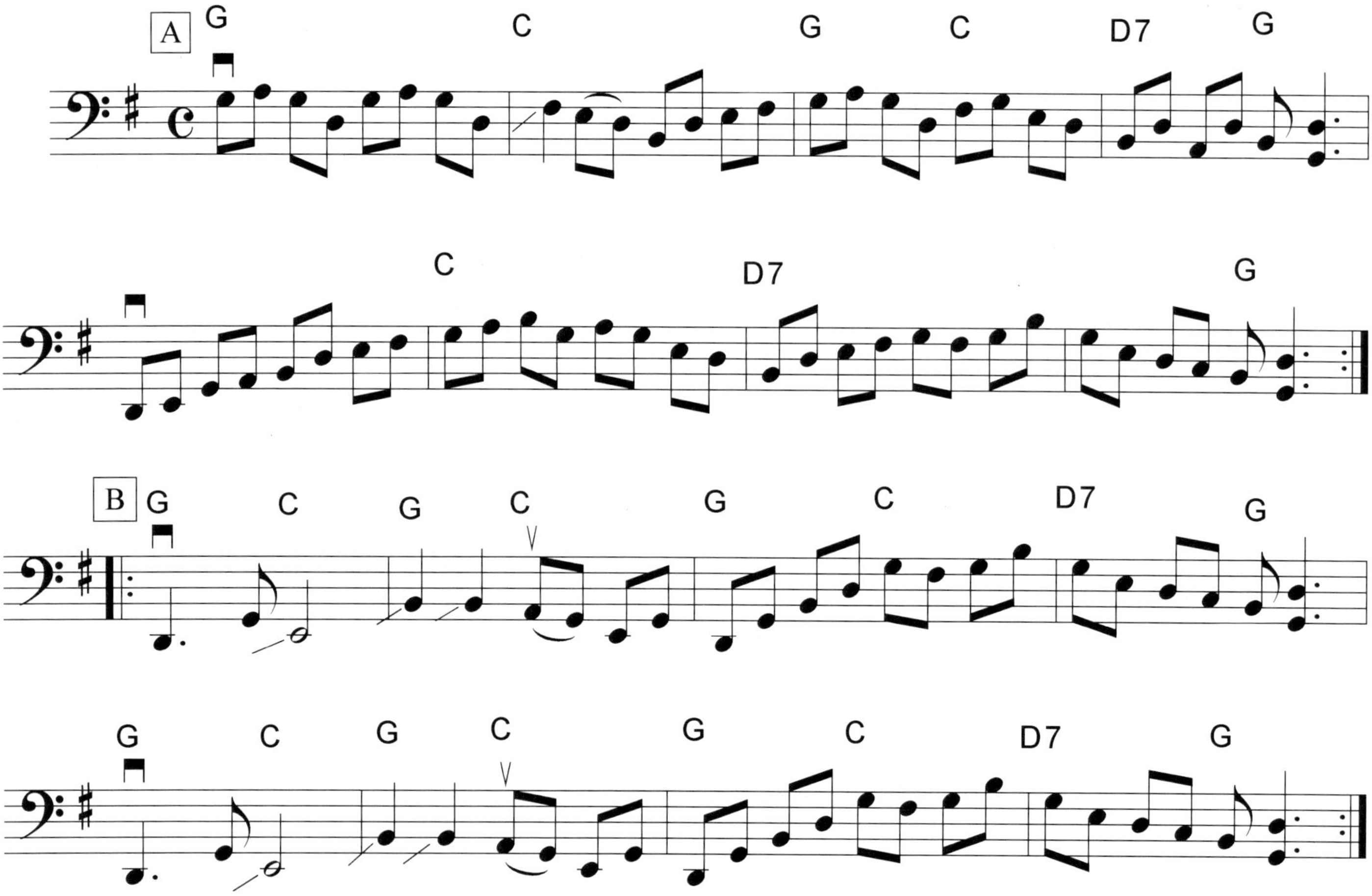

# Fisher's Hornpipe

23

This version has been modified to simplify the fingering.

Straight or swing rhythm
Fast tempo

Traditional

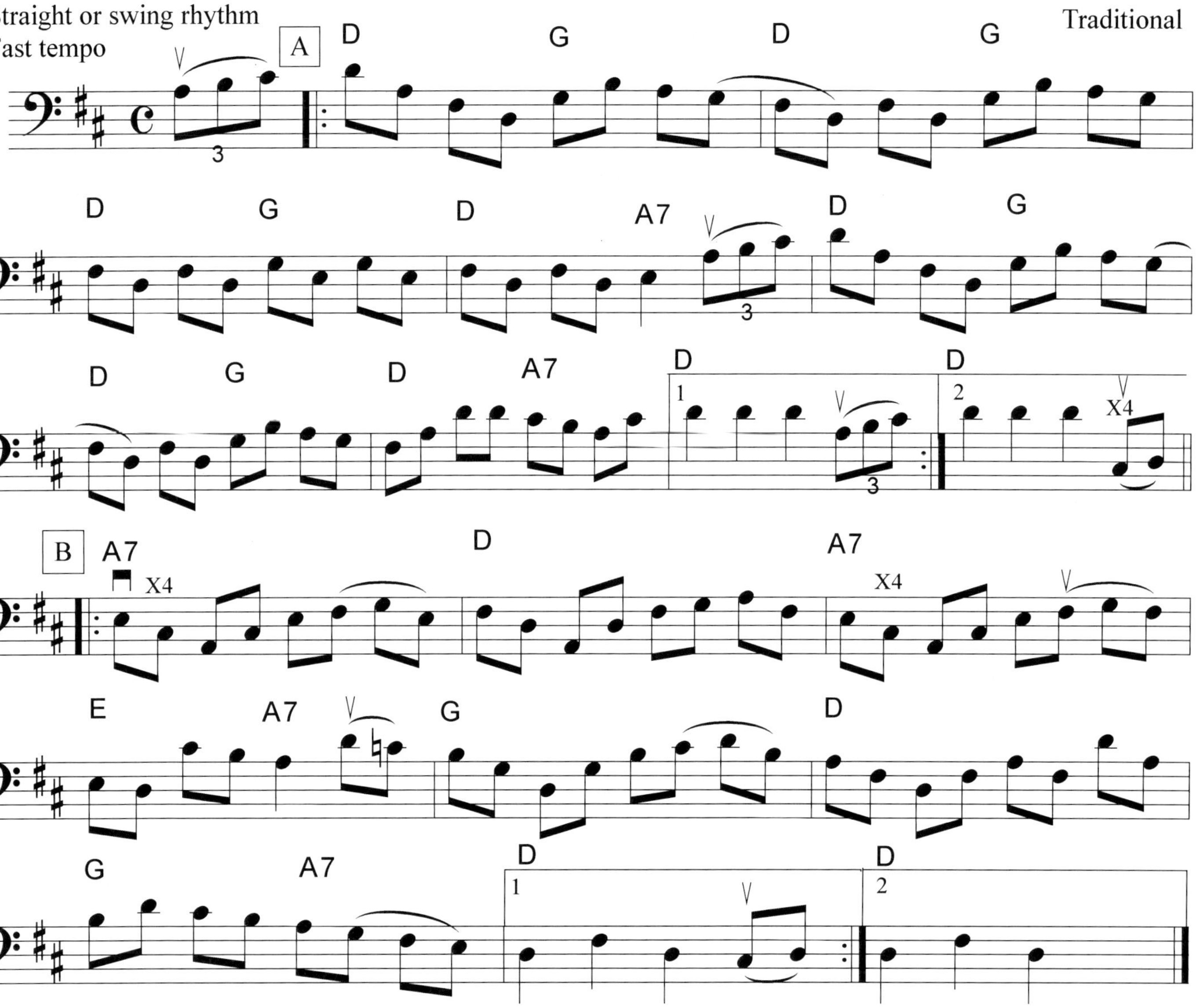


The B part using extended position.

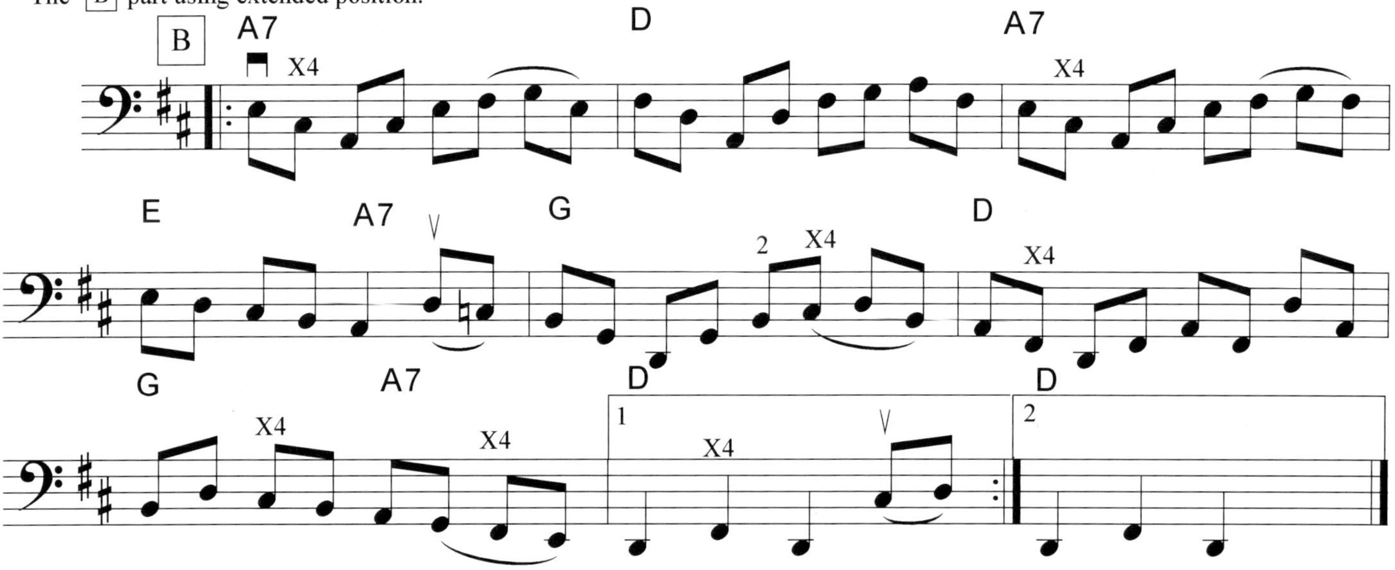

24

# Teetotaler's Reel

(Simplified)

Straight rhythm
Fast or moderate tempo

This version has been modified to simplify the fingering.

Traditional

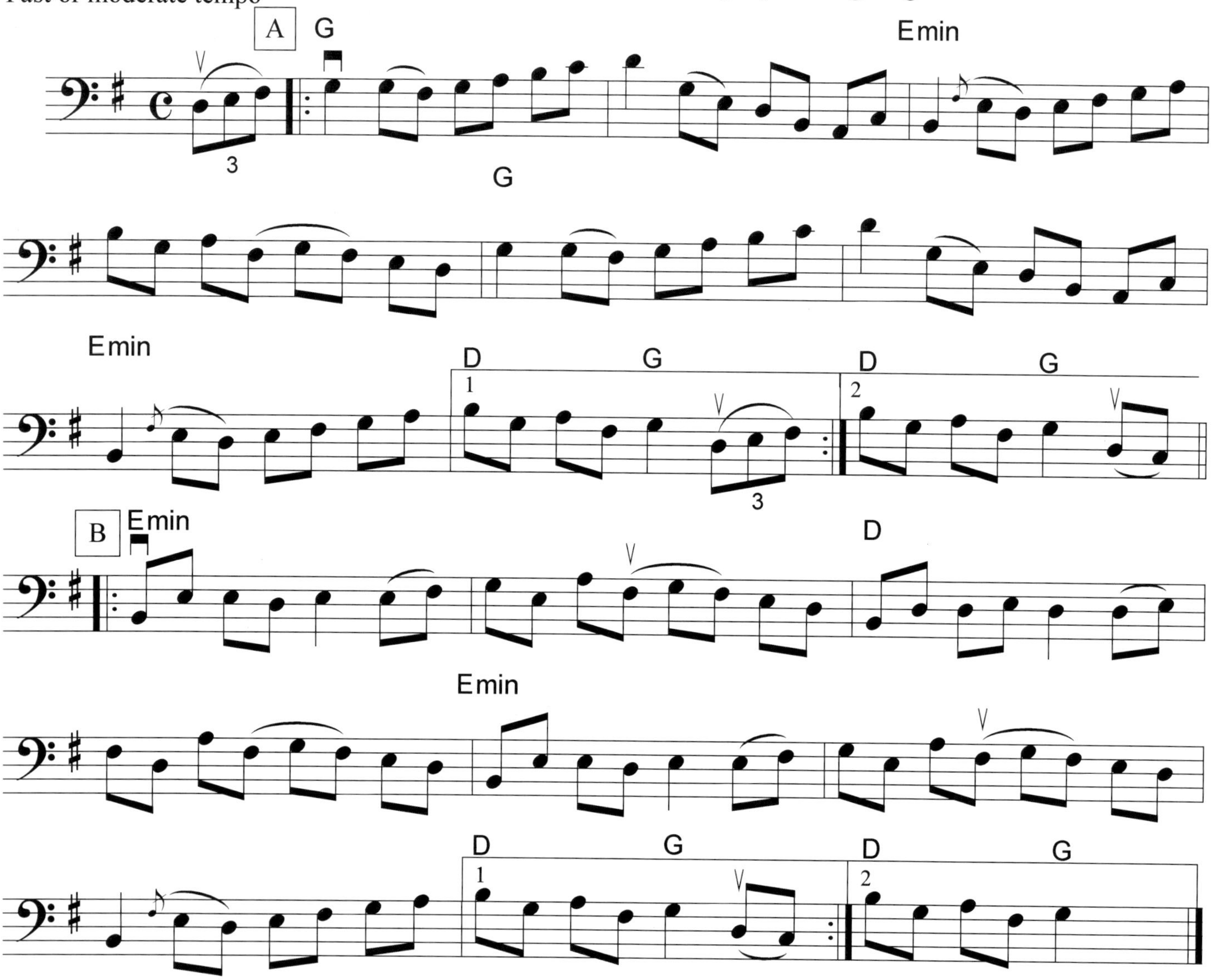


The [A] part with shifting.

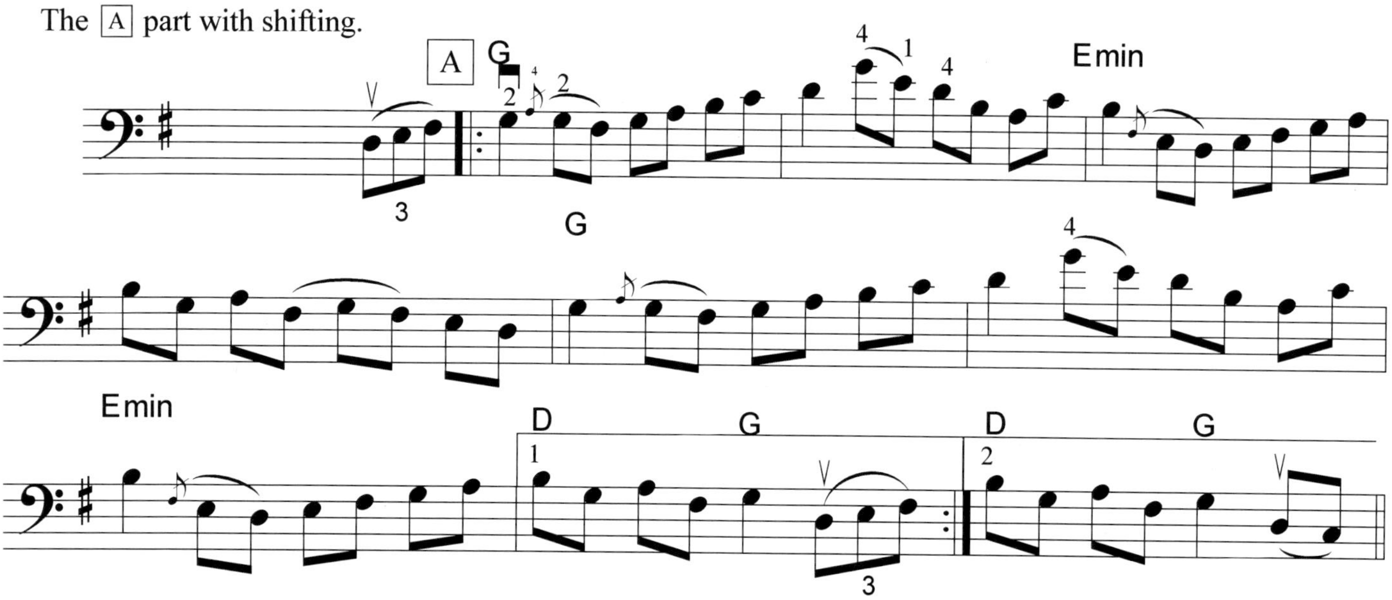

25

# Temperance Reel

(Simplified)

The "Teetotaler's Reel" and "Temperance Reel" are two different versions of the same tune which is also known as "Kingsport" or "The Devil in Georgia". The two different versions can represent the contrast in styles of fiddling. "Temperance Reel" has some added variation to give it a different sound. Be sure to swing the rhythm.

Swing rhythm
Fast or moderate tempo

Traditional

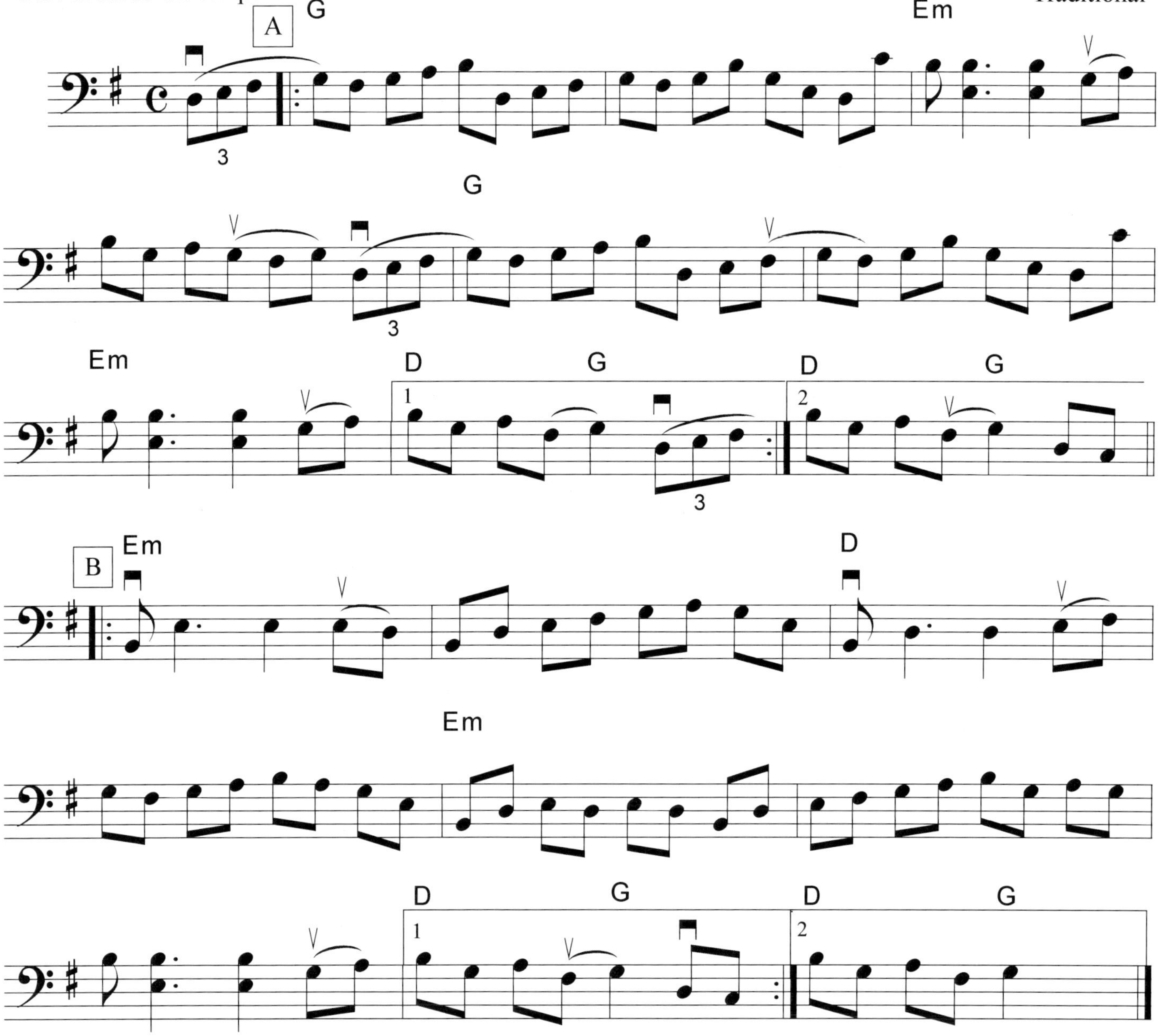

26

# Ragtime Annie

This version is modified to simplify the fingering.

Straight rhythm
Fast or moderate tempo

Traditional

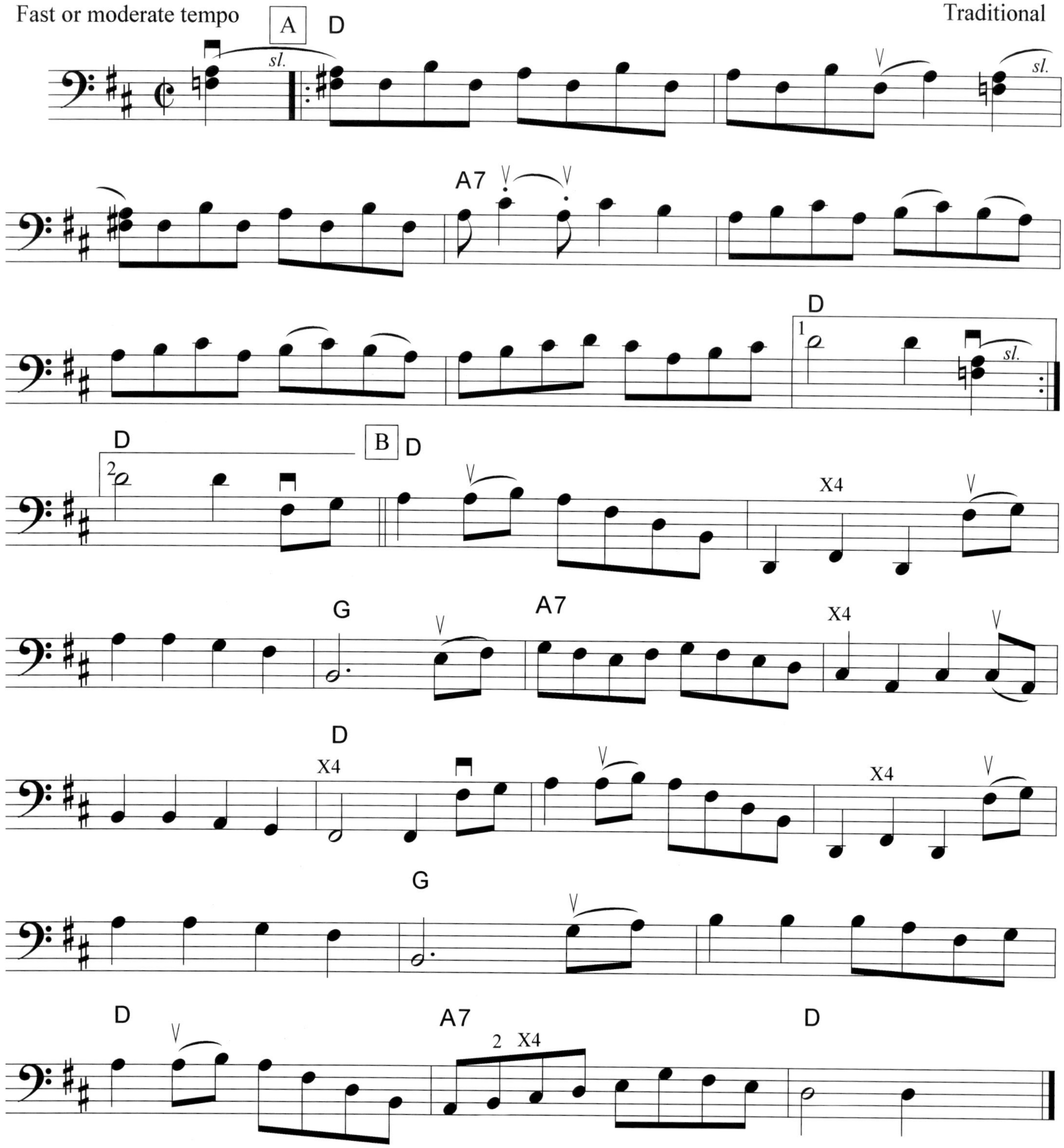

# Crazy Creek

"Crazy Creek," which has a very unique sound is best known as a bluegrass instrumental.

Swing rhythm
Fast or moderate tempo

Attributed to
Tommy Jackson

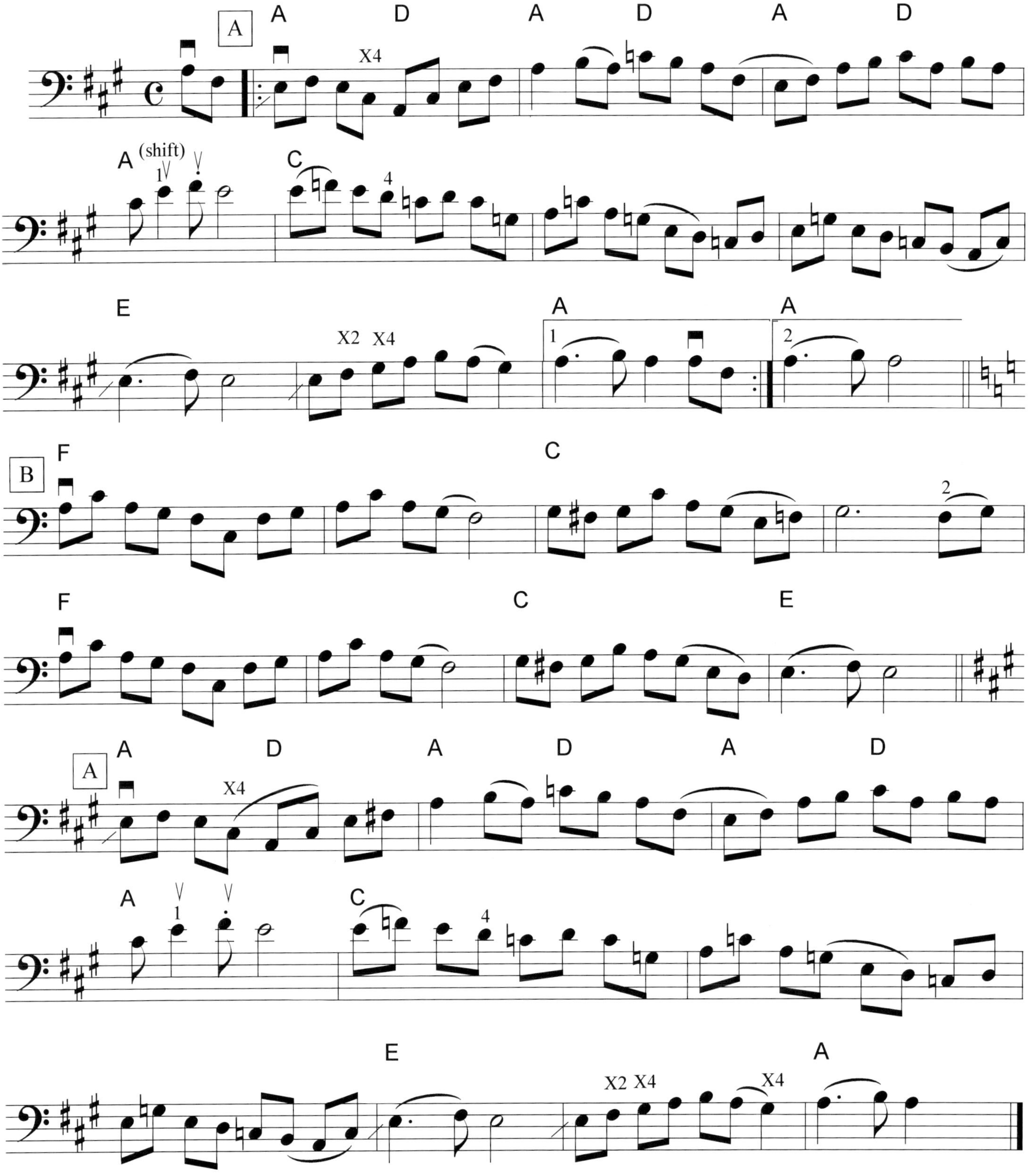

28

# Ook Pik Waltz

(Simplified)

Swing rhythm on eighth notes
Danceable waltz tempo

This version is modified to simplify the fingering.

Frankie Rodgers

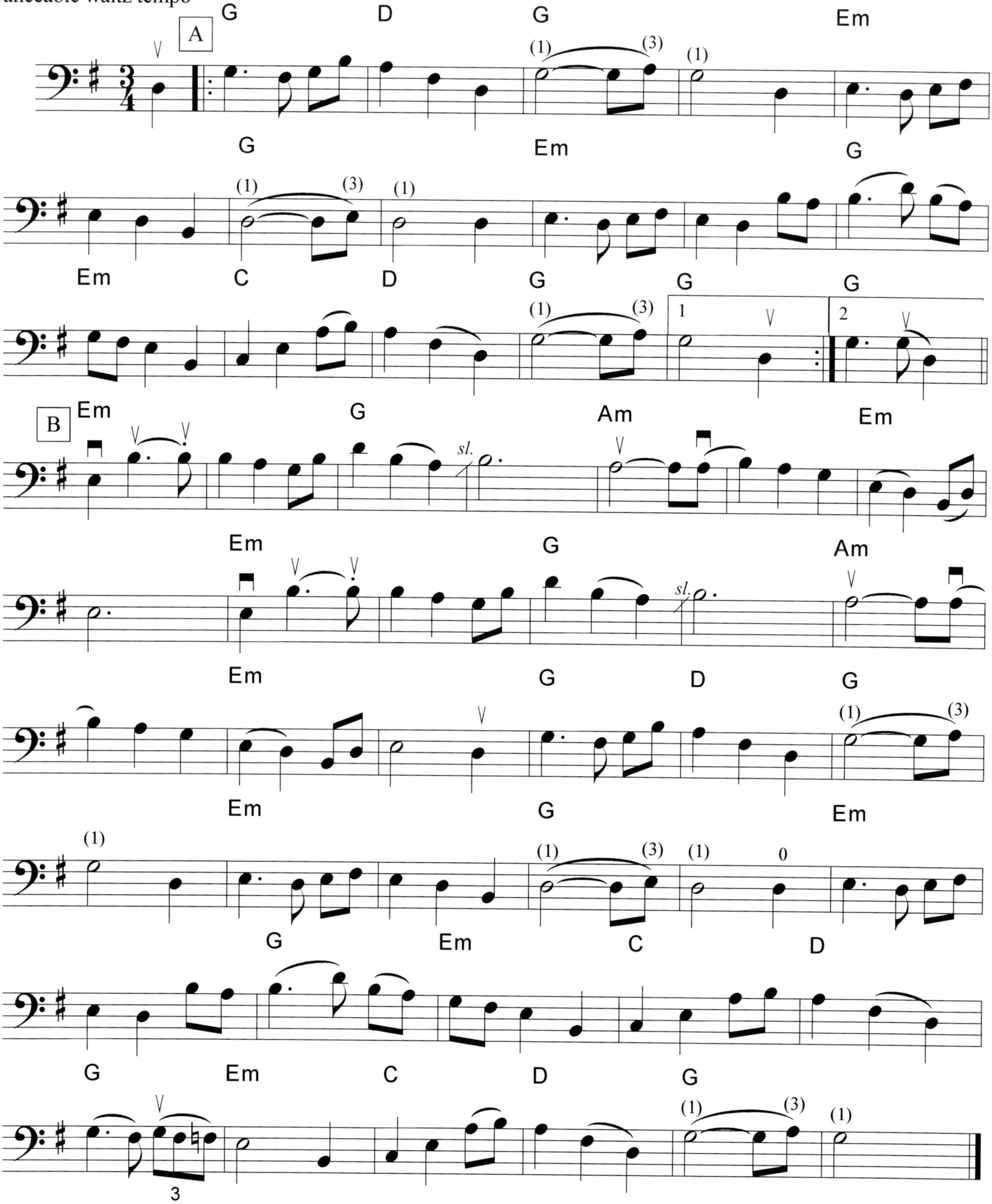

29

# Ook Pik Waltz

(Original version)

Swing rhythm on eighth notes
Danceable waltz tempo

Frankie Rodgers

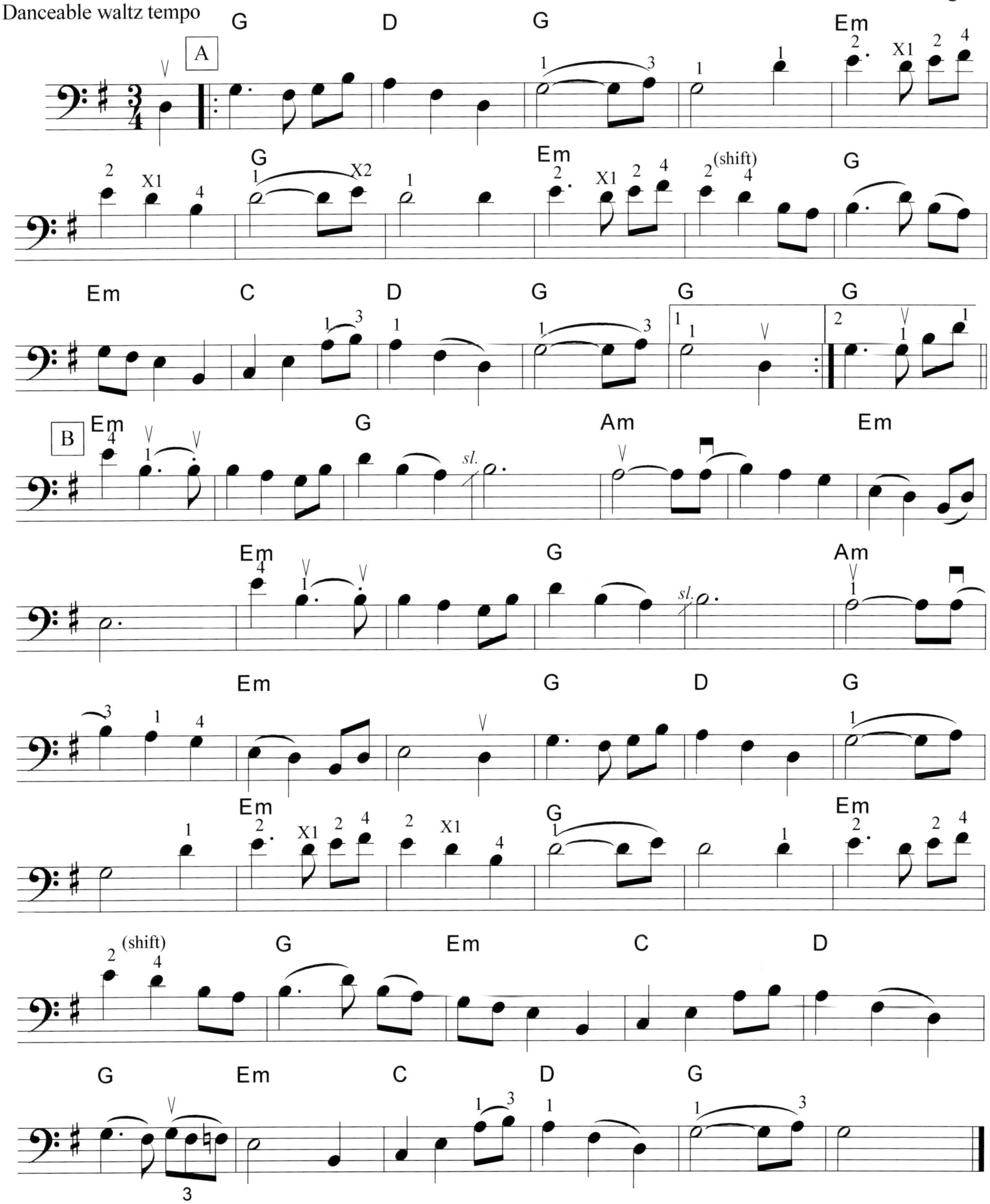

30

# Goodnight Waltz

This version is modified to simplify the fingering. The guitar chords marked in parentheses are optional chords which can be added for more variety.

Swing rhythm on eighth notes
Danceable waltz tempo

Traditional

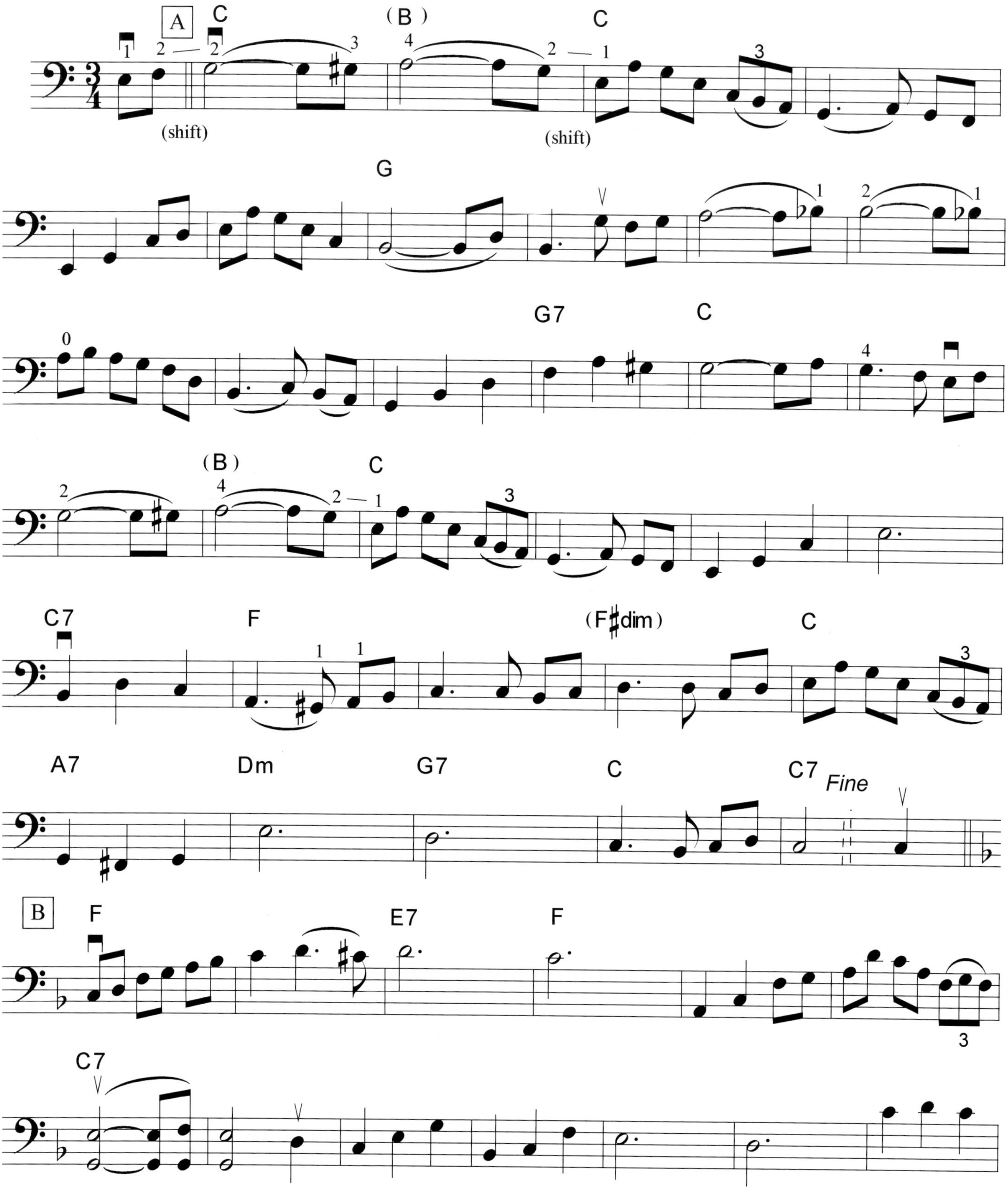

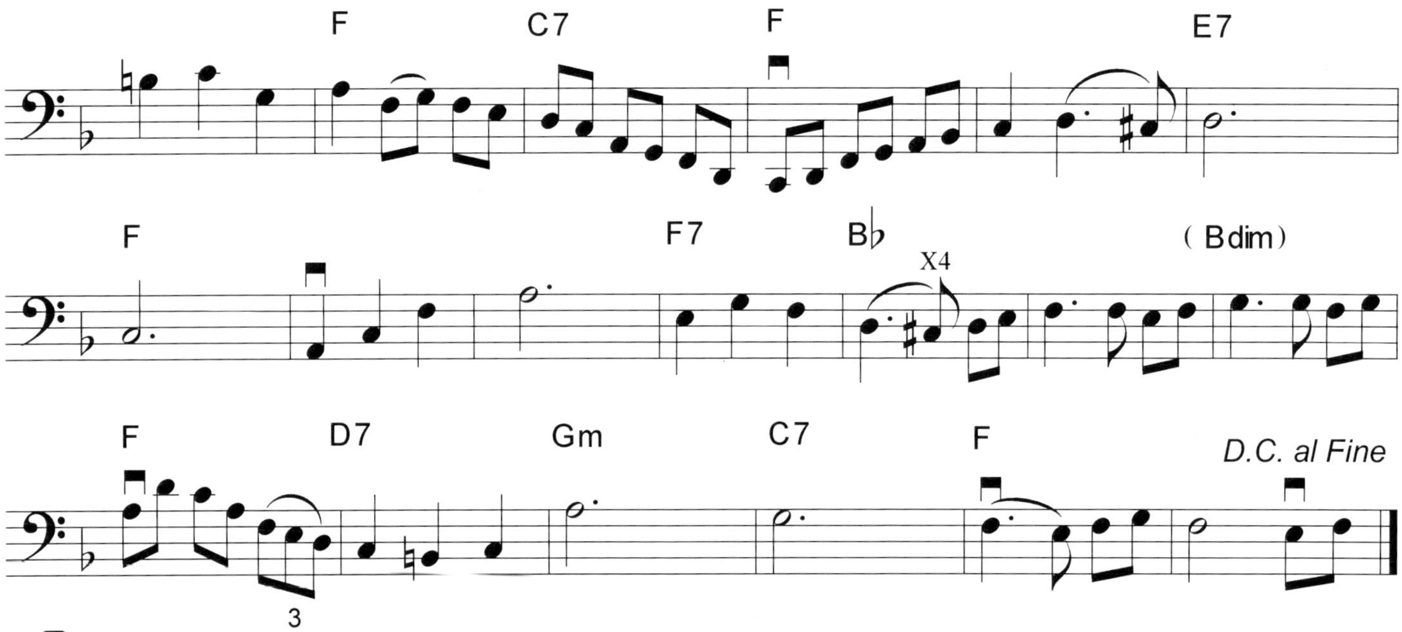


31 The B section with shifting.

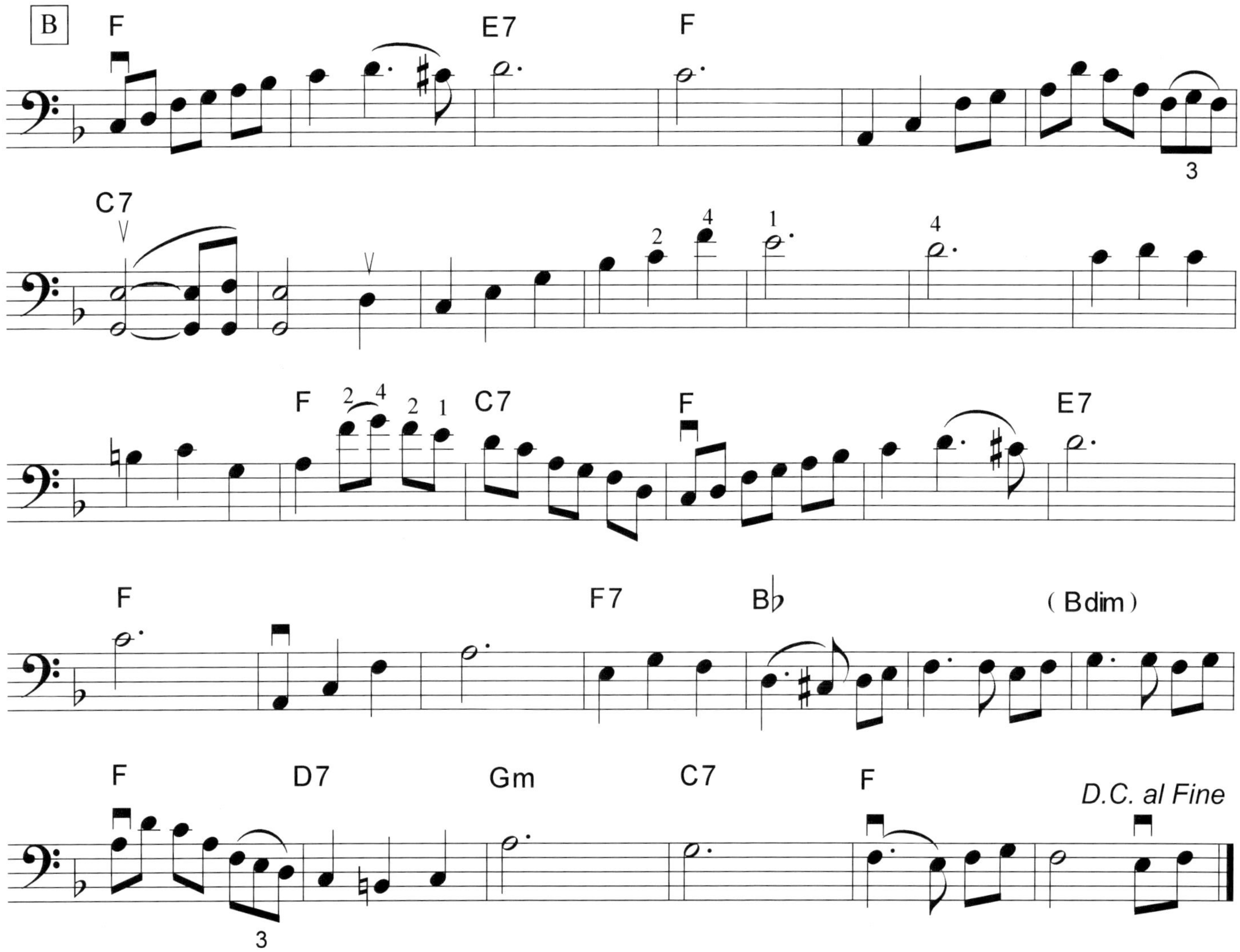

32

# Angus Campbell

(Simplified)

Swing rhythm
Fast or moderate tempo

This version is modified to simplify the fingering.

Traditional

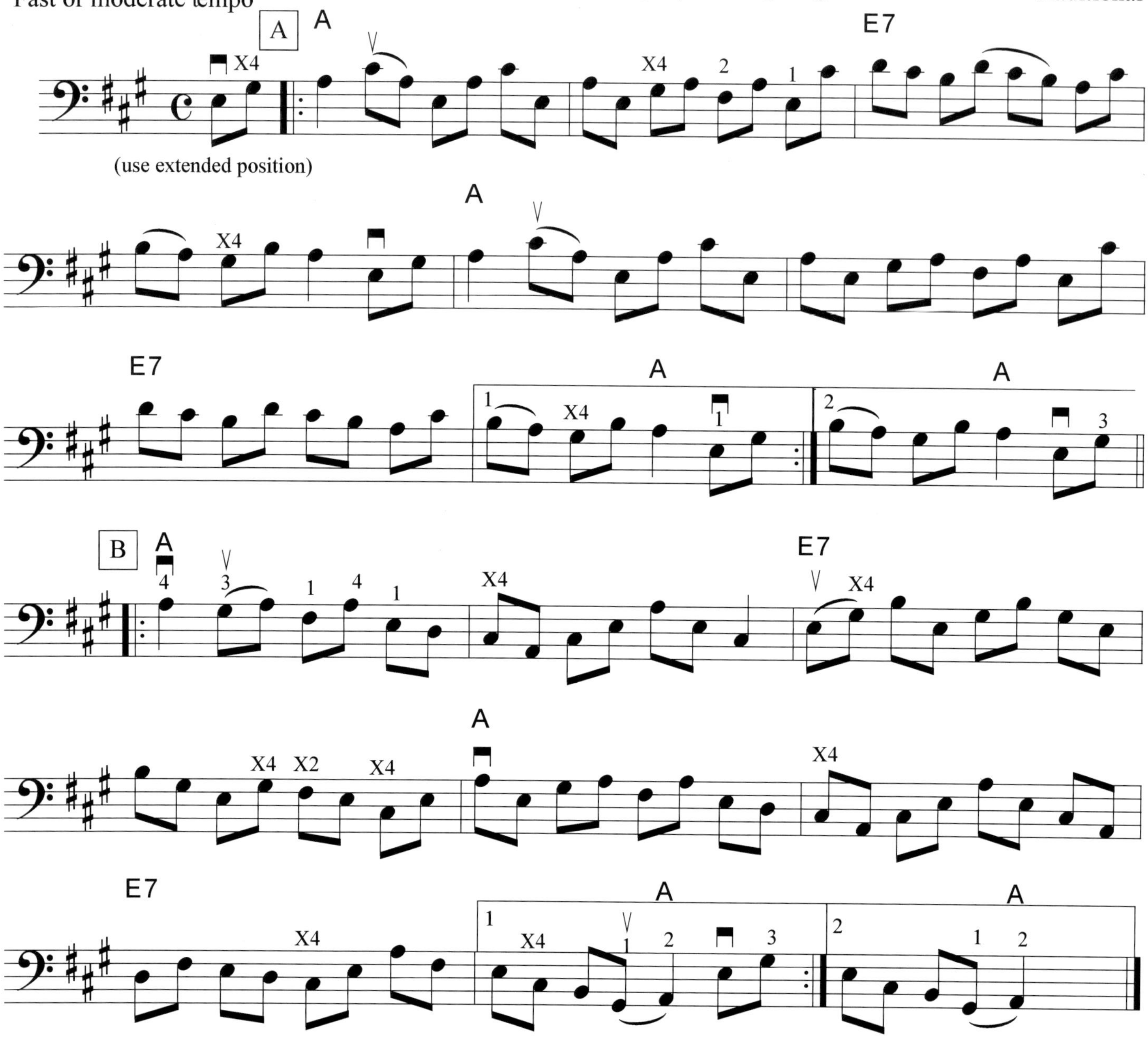


## Texas-Style Fiddling

Texas-style fiddling is a distinct style that brings elements of swing and jazz into traditional oldtime fiddle tunes. A player improvises passages of the tune to add variety. Players also listen to each other and mimic each other's playing. The style began in Texas with players such as Major Franklin, Lewis Franklin, Vernon Solomon and Benny Thomason. Benny Thomason helped introduce the style to contests like the Weiser National Oldtime Fiddler's Contest, and he taught many young fiddlers.

The following tunes are often played among Texas-style fiddlers and in fiddle contests. The versions are basic and have workable bowings.

33

# Angus Campbell

(Lower, original version)

Swing rhythm
Fast or moderate tempo

Traditional

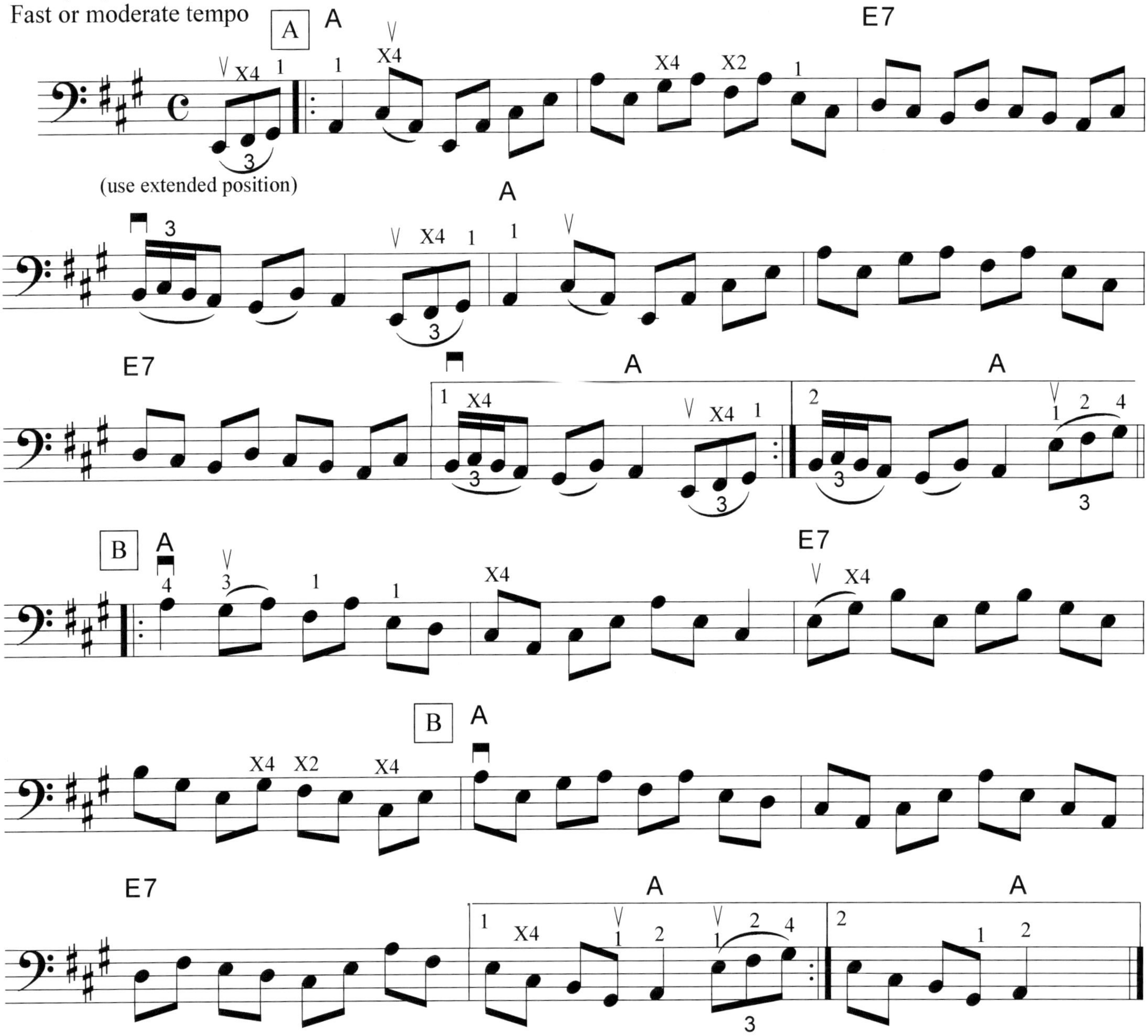

34

# Bill Cheatum

(Simplified)

Swing rhythm
Fast or moderate tempo

This version is modified to simplify the fingering.

Traditional

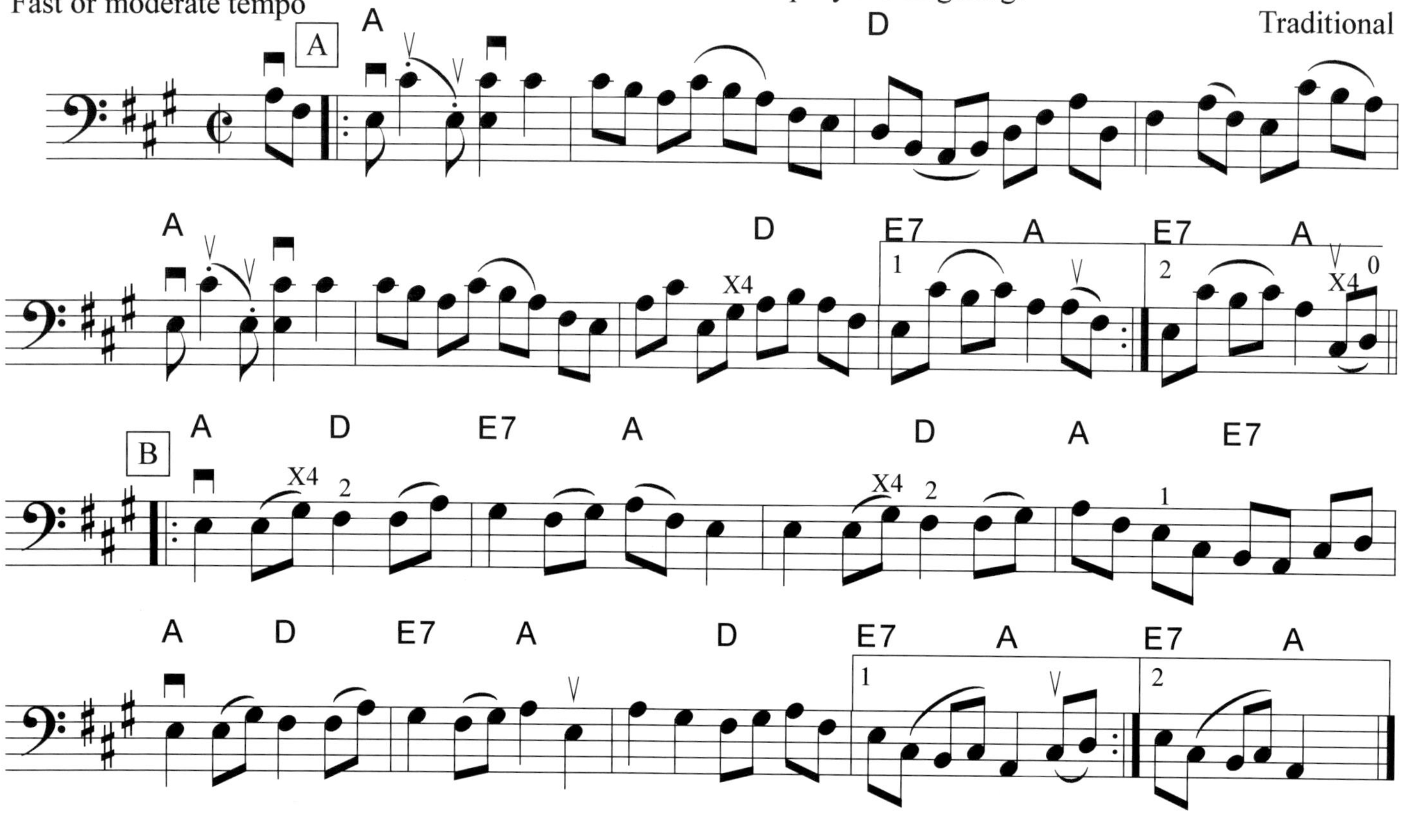


35

# Bill Cheatum

(Original version)

Swing rhythm
Fast or moderate tempo

Traditional

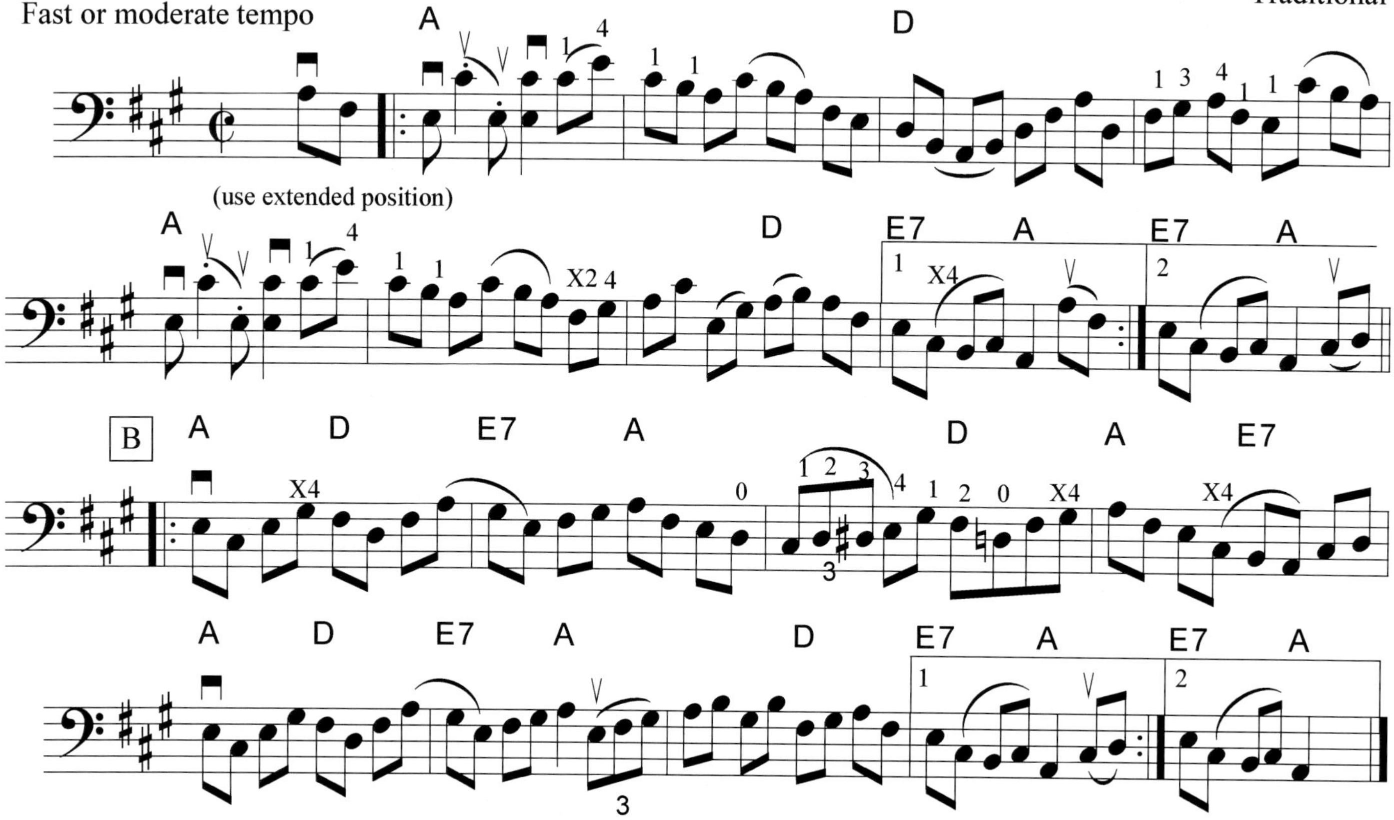

36

# Forester's Reel

(Simplified)

Swing rhythm
Fast or moderate tempo

This version has been modified to simplify the fingering.

Traditional

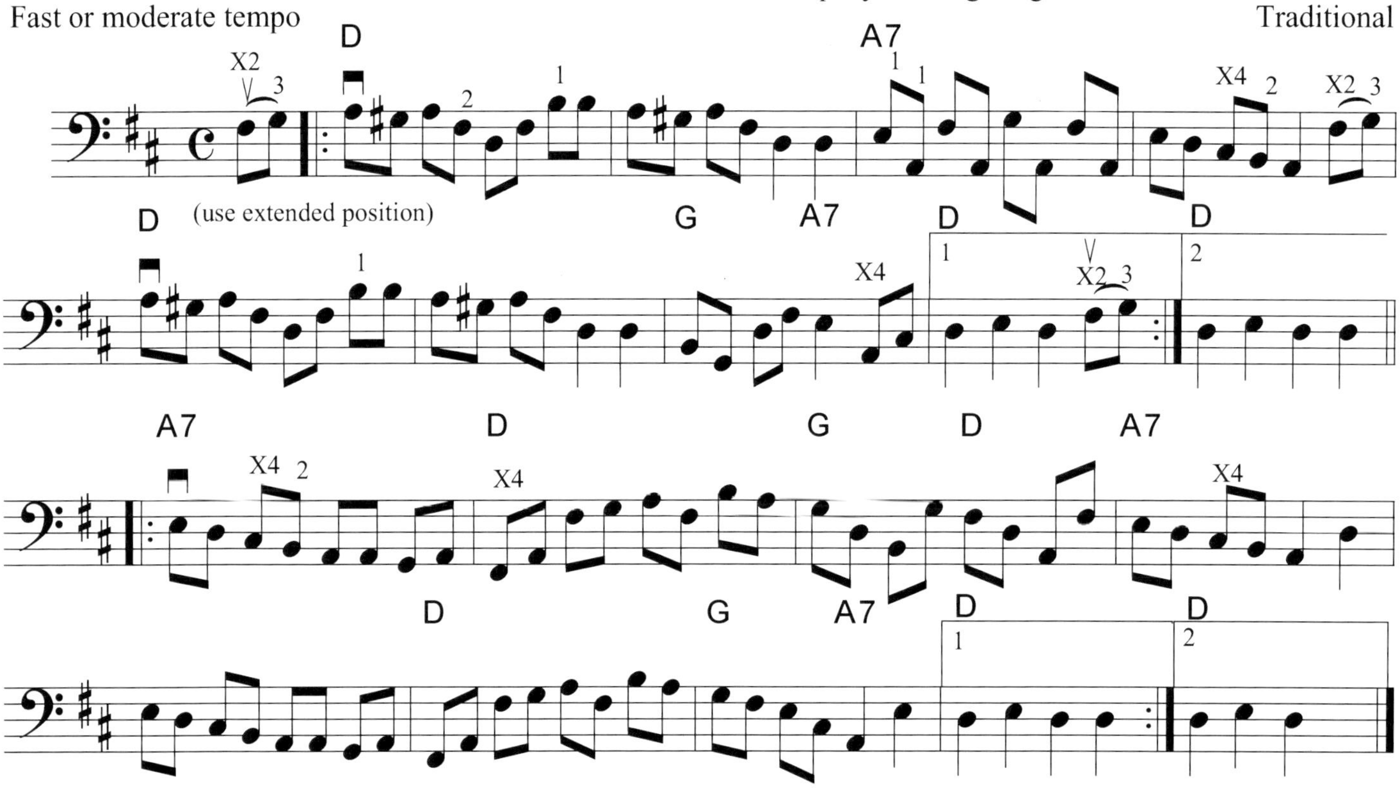


37

# Forester's Reel

(Original version)

Swing rhythm

Traditional

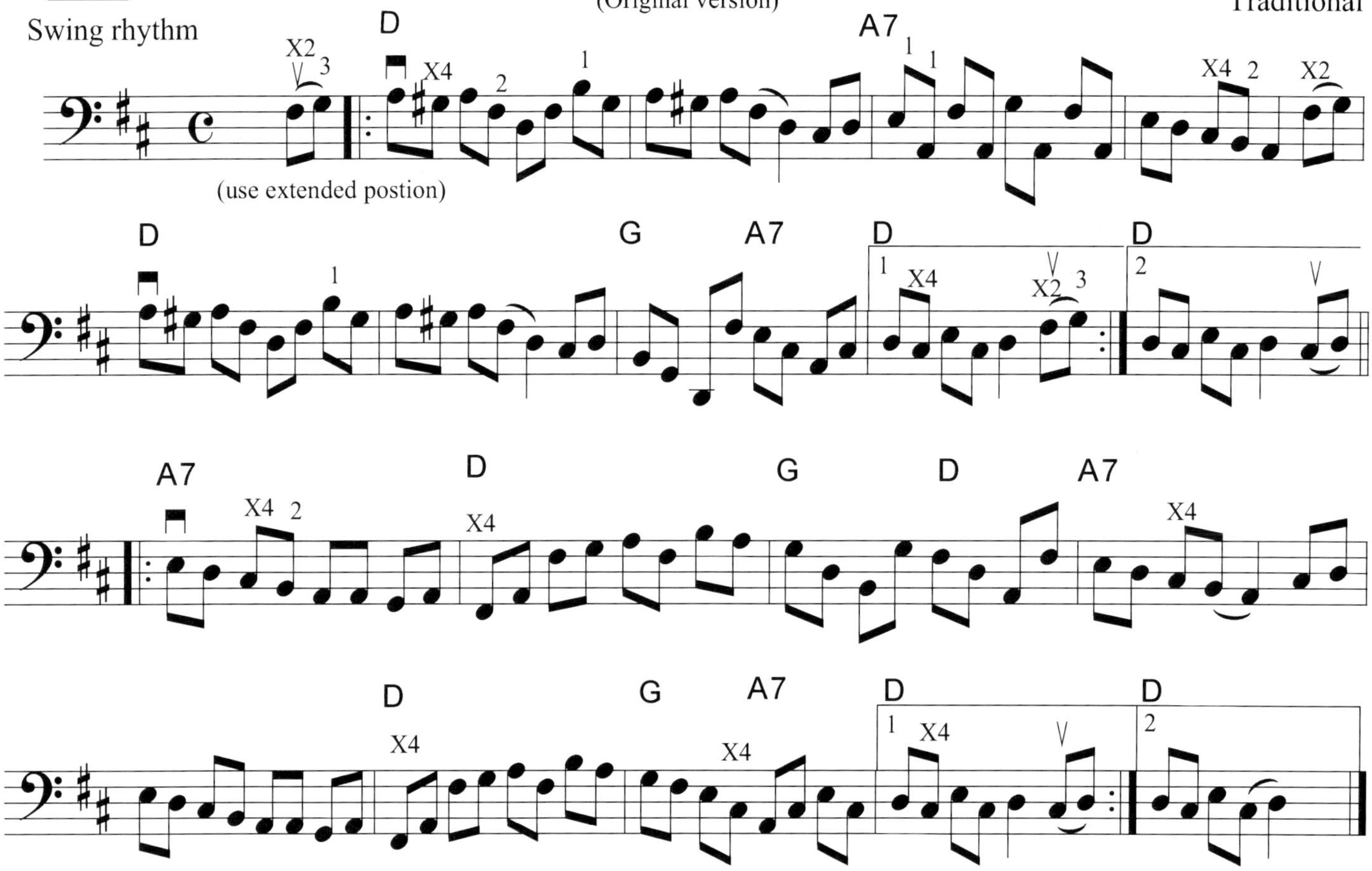

38

# New Broom

Swing rhythm
Fast or moderate tempo

Traditional

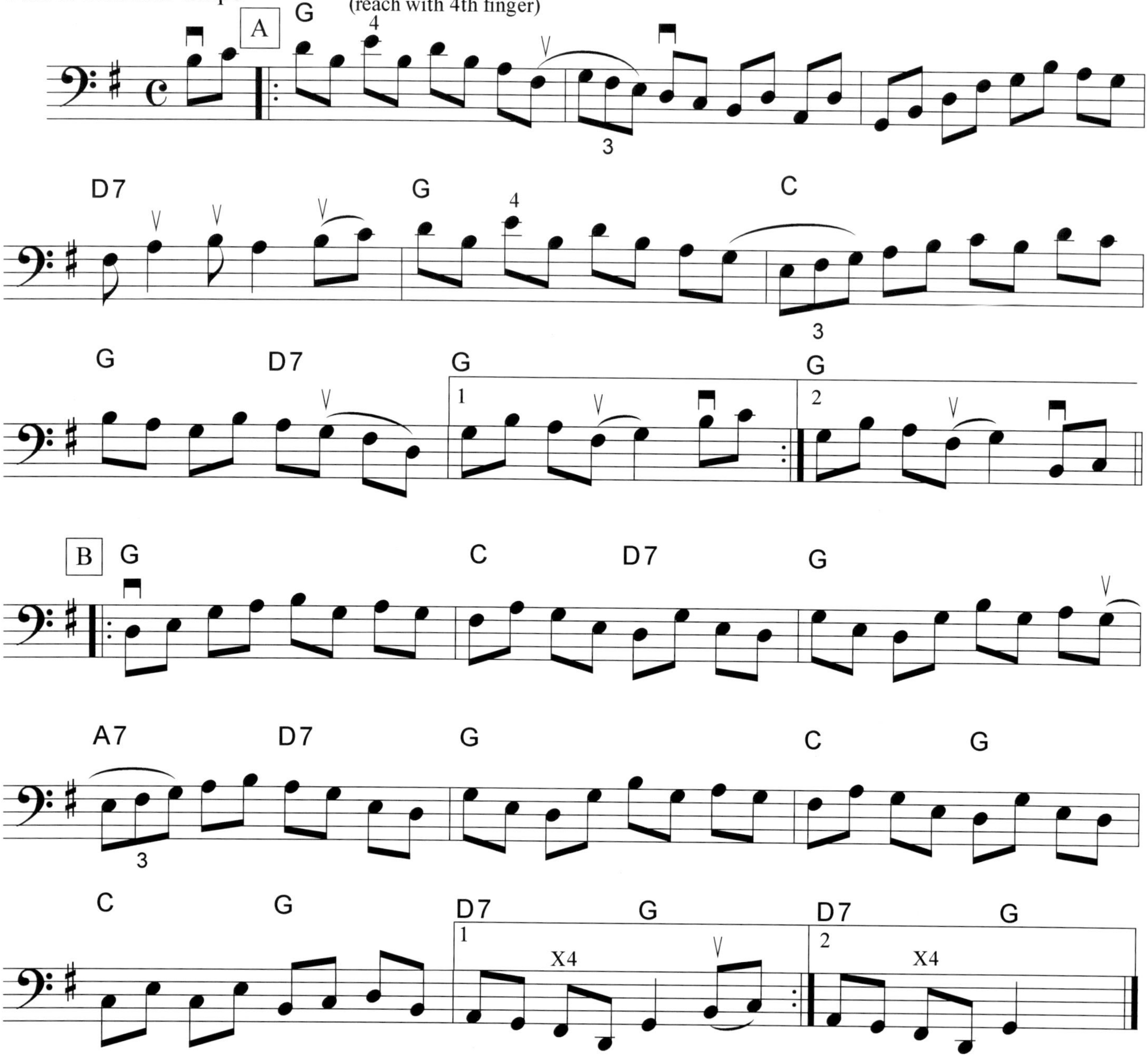

# Snowflake Reel

This version has been modified to simplify the fingering.

Attributed to
Wally Traugott

Swing rhythm
Fast or moderate tempo

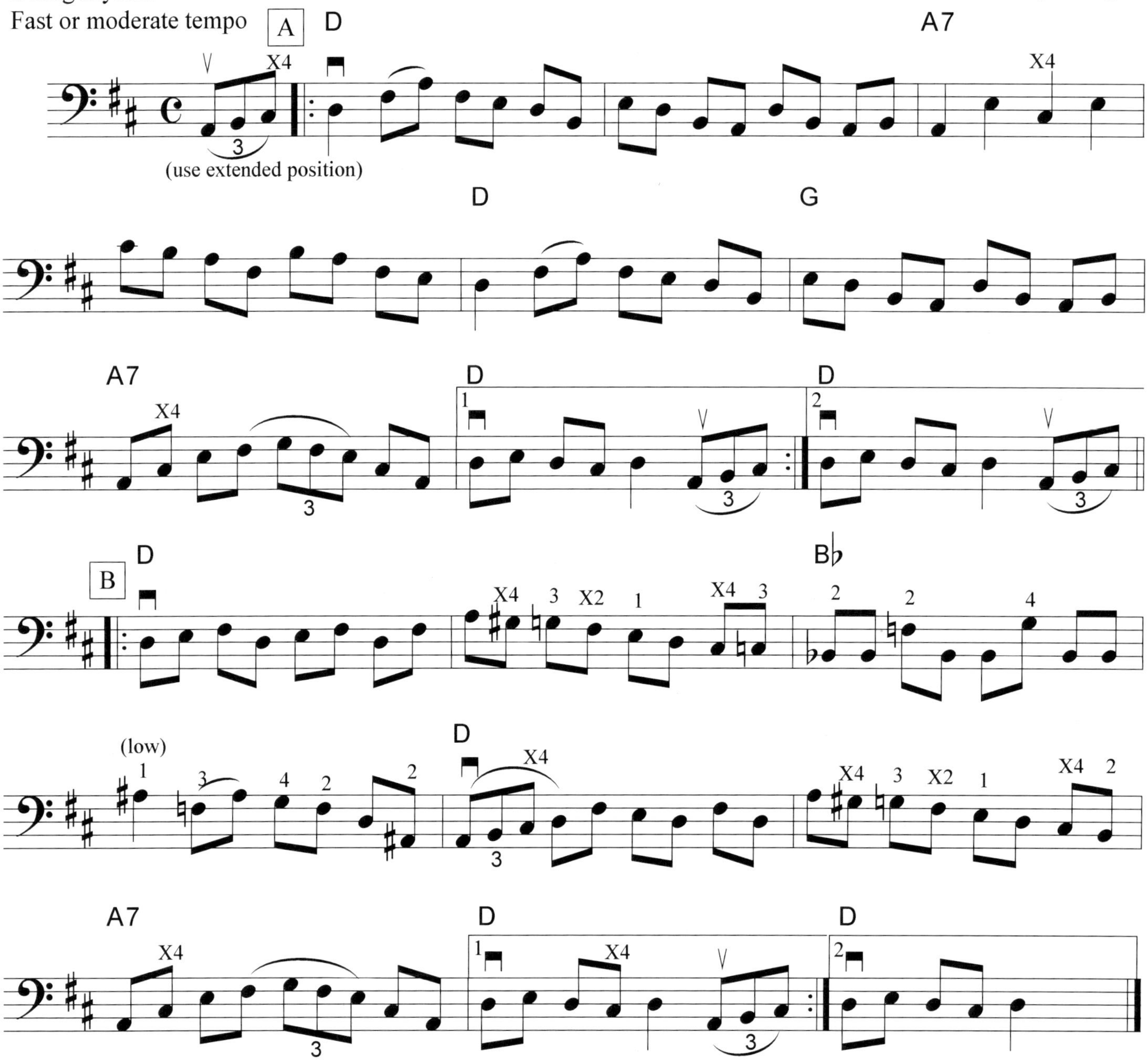

40

# Cuckoo's Nest 1

(Simplified)

Several versions of "Cuckoo's Nest" are given here to show options for fingering and contrast in styles. This version has been modified to simplify the fingering.

Swing rhythm
Moderate tempo

Traditional

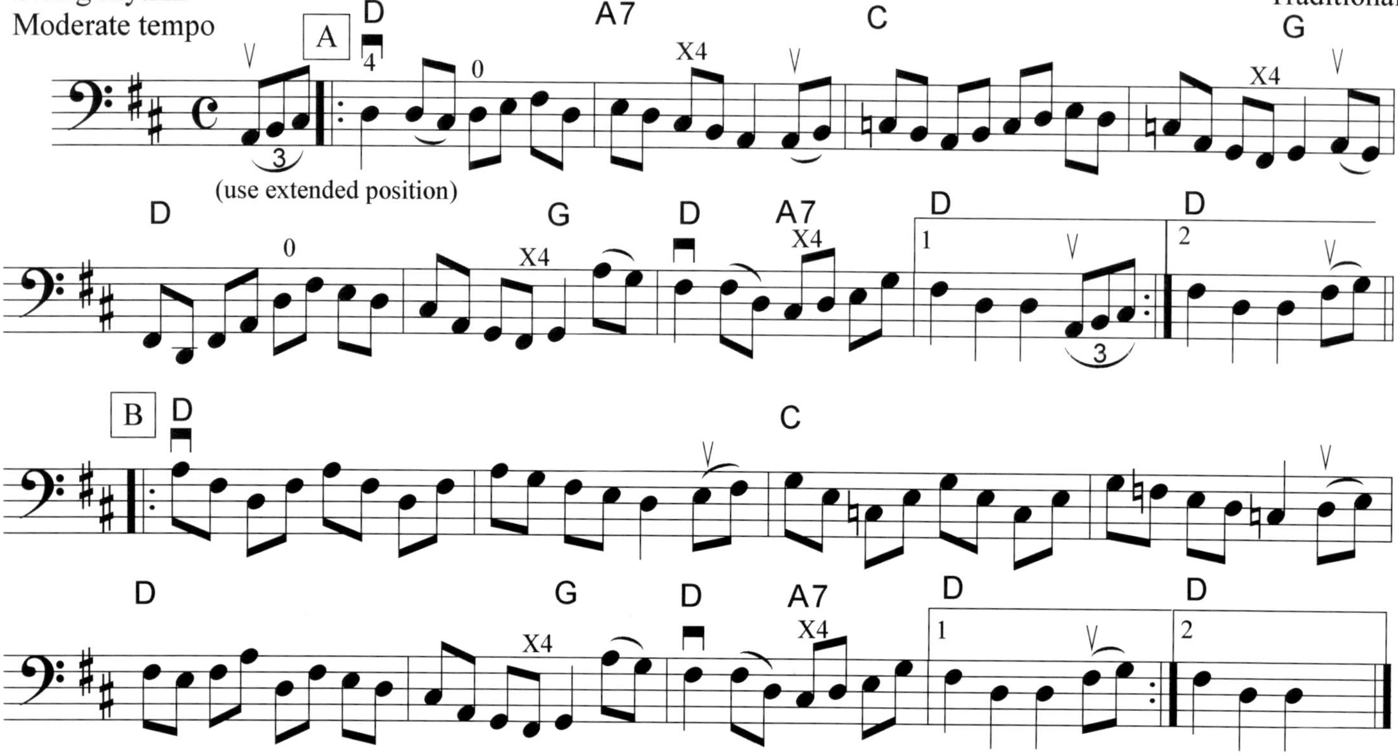


41

# Cuckoo's Nest 1

(Original version)

Swing rhythm

Traditional

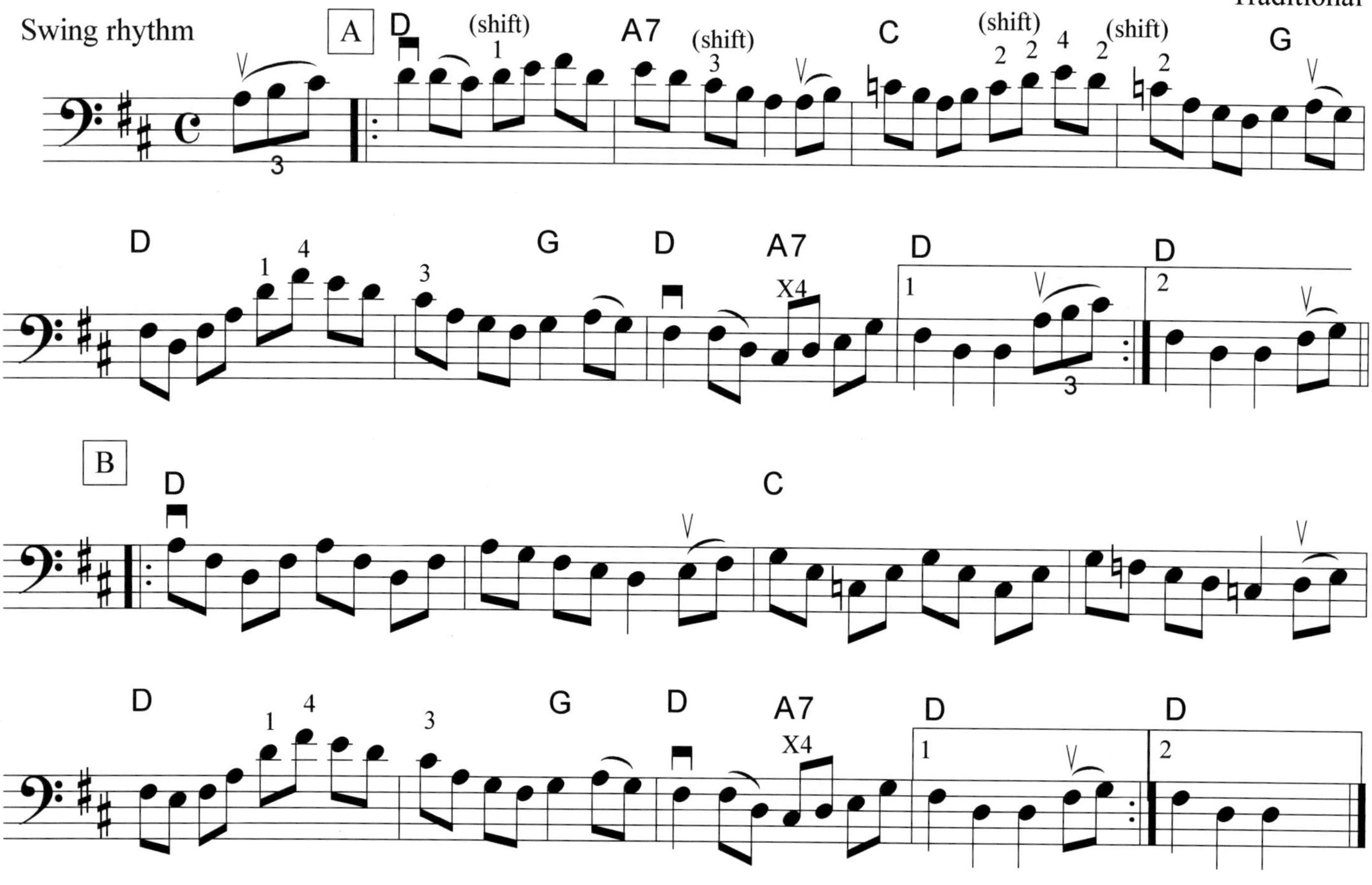

42

# Cuckoo's Nest 2

(Simplified)

This version of "Cuckoo's Nest" shows how a tune can be played in different ways.
This version uses more lower strings without shifting and slightly different note patterns.

Traditional

Swing rhythm
Moderate tempo

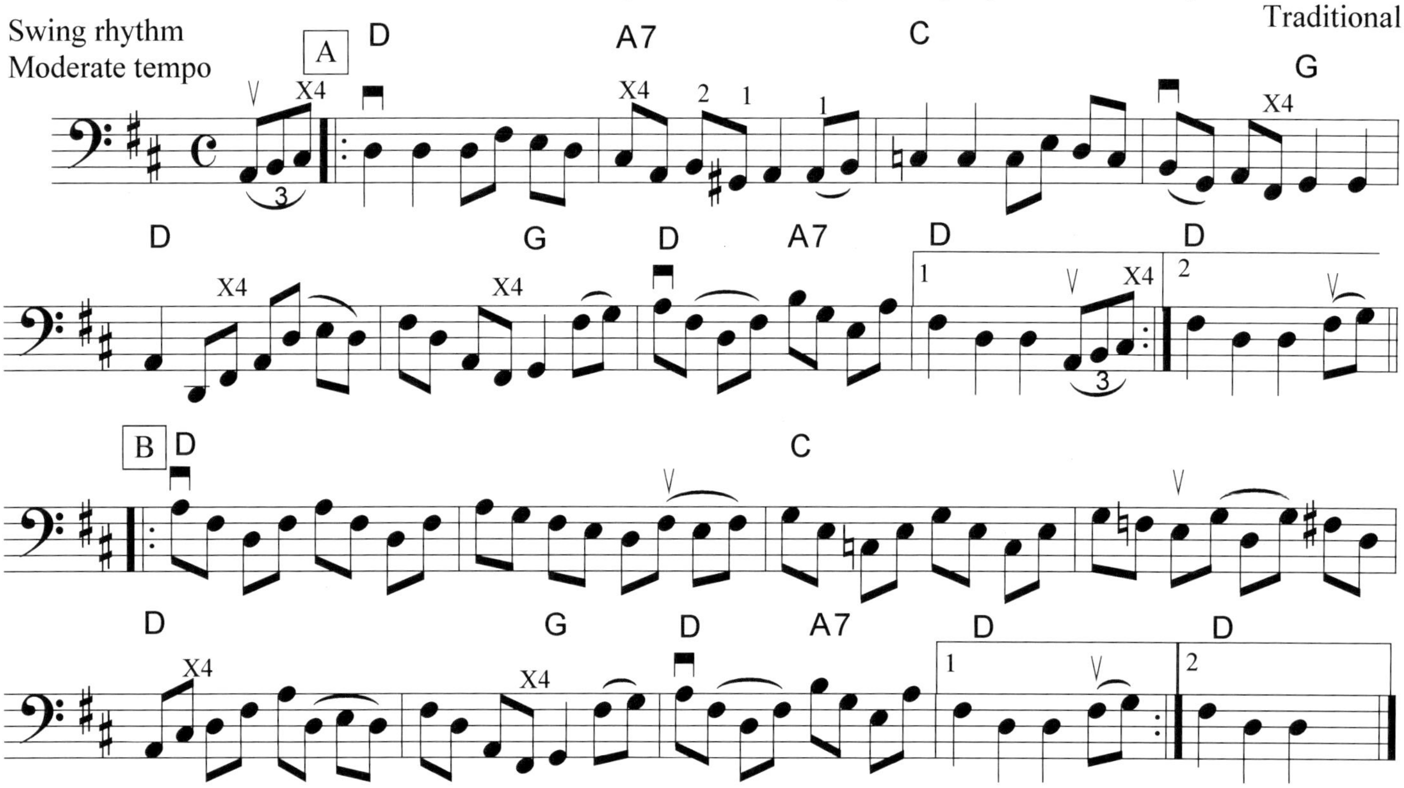

43

# Cuckoo's Nest 2

(Variation with shifting)

Traditional

Swing rhythm

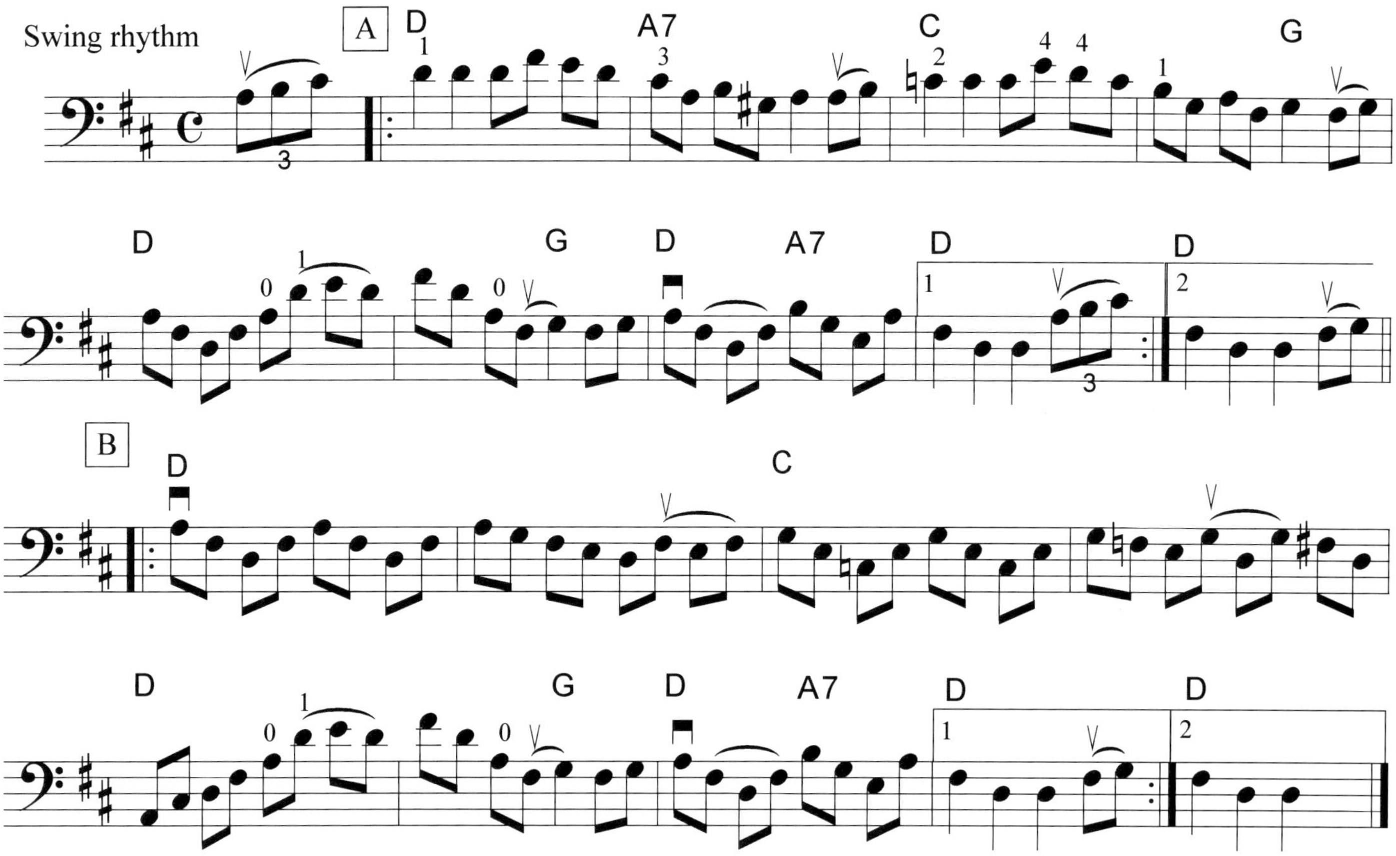

44

# Snowshoes

(Simplified)

Swing rhythm
Fast or moderate tempo

This version has been modified to simplify the fingering.

Traditional

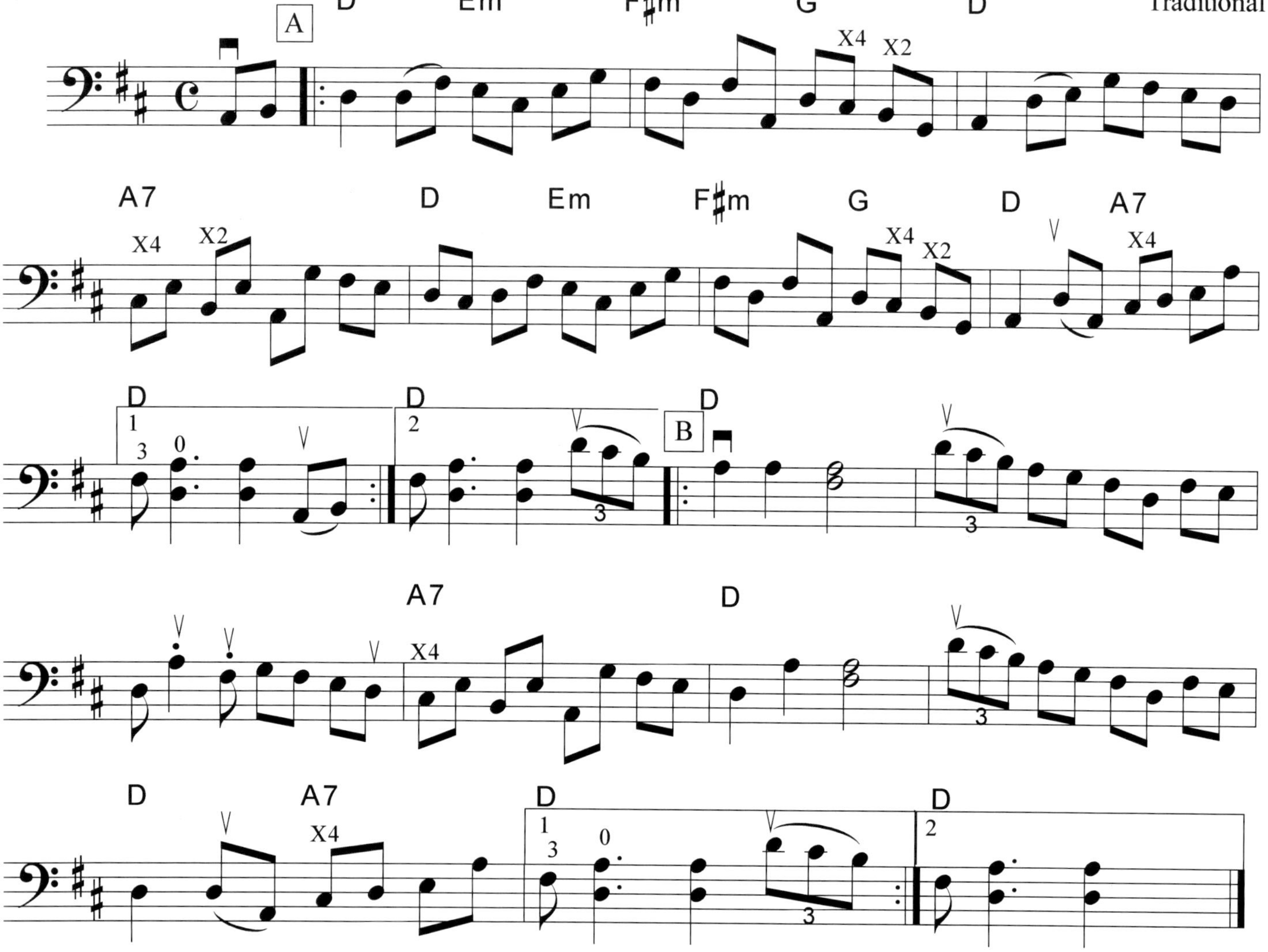

45

# Forked Deer

Swing rhythm
Moderate tempo

Traditional

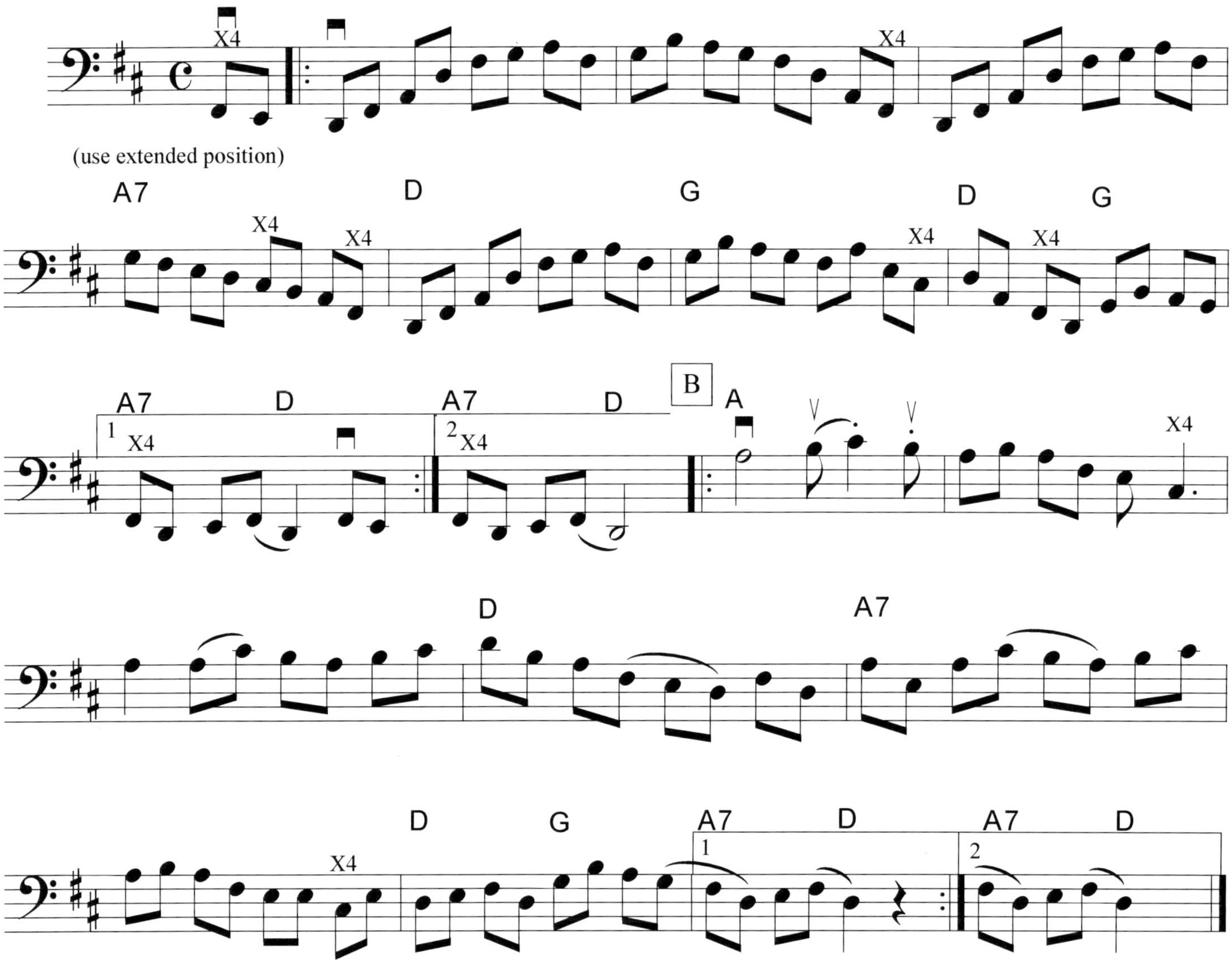

46

# Bittercreek

Swing rhythm
Fast or moderate tempo

This version has been modified to simiplify the fingering.

Traditional

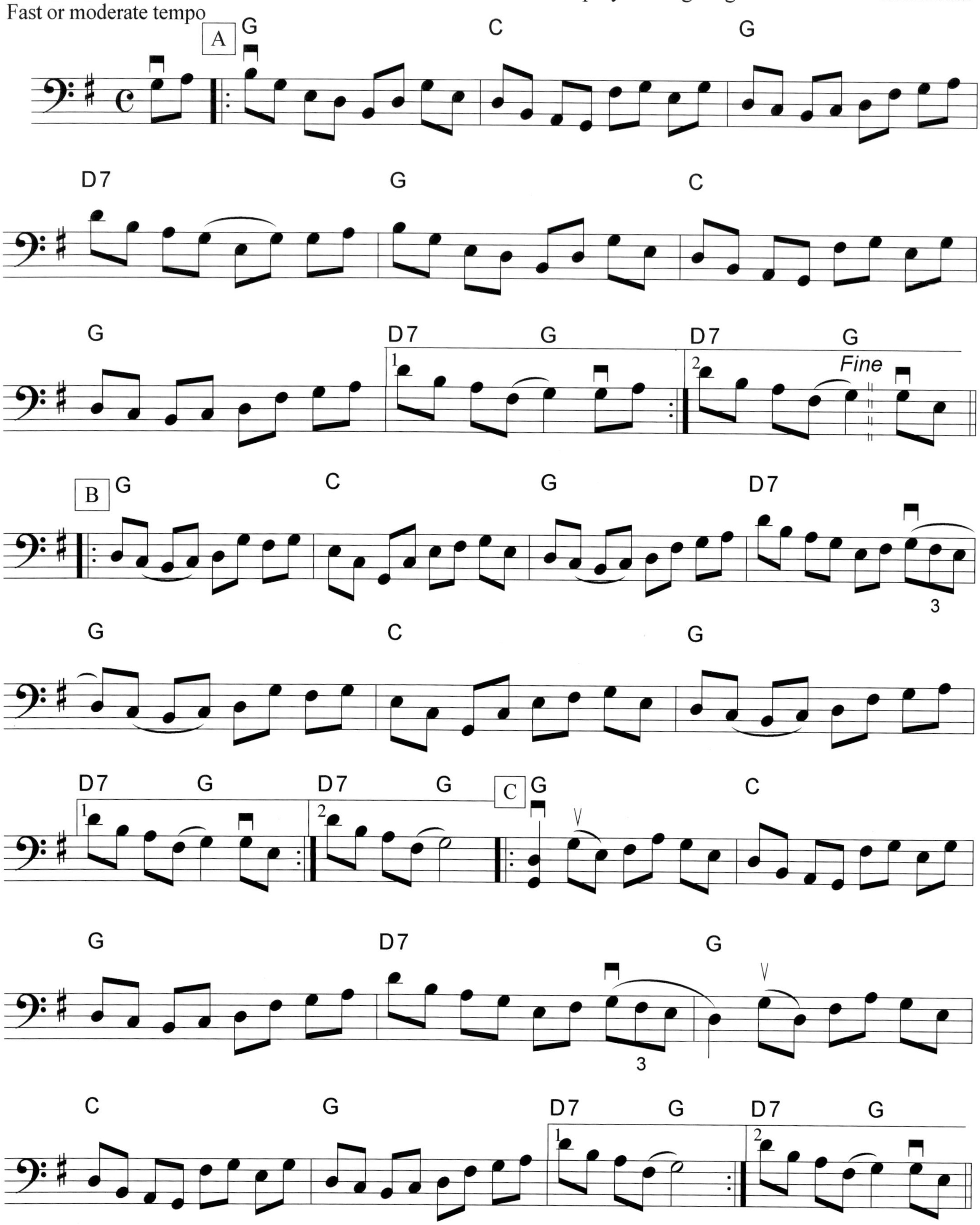

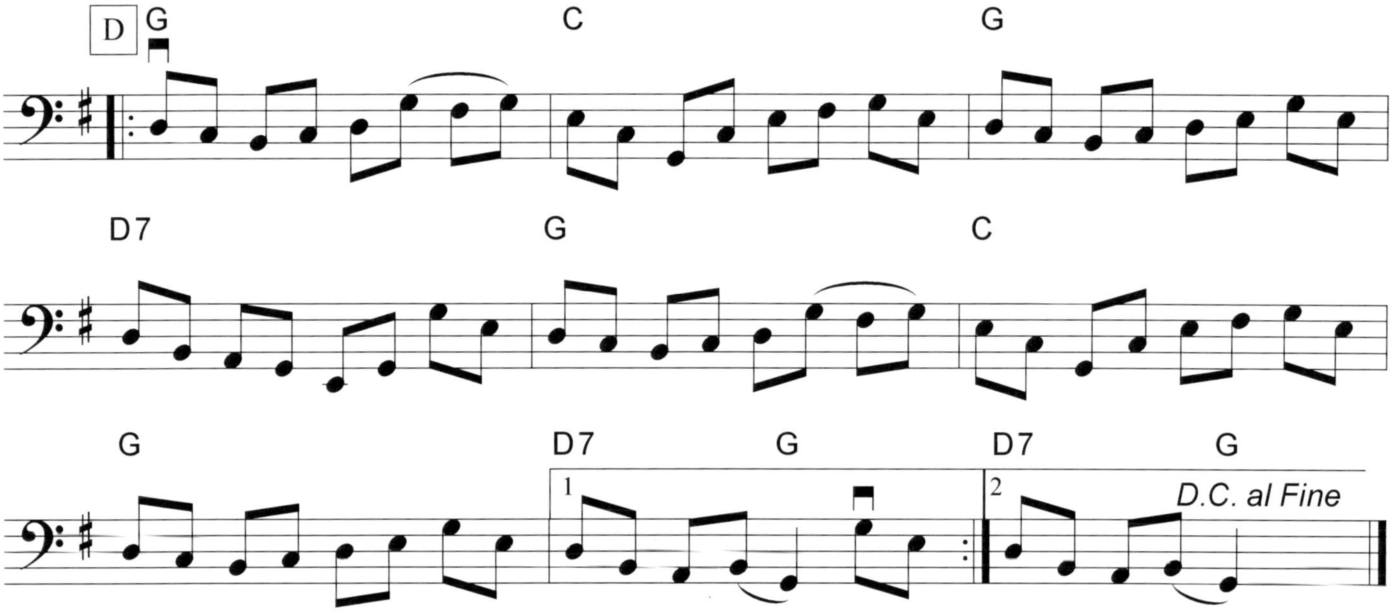
D
G
C
G
D7
G
C
G
D7
G
1
D7
G
2
D.C. al Fine

47

# Salt River

This version has been modified to simplify the fingering.

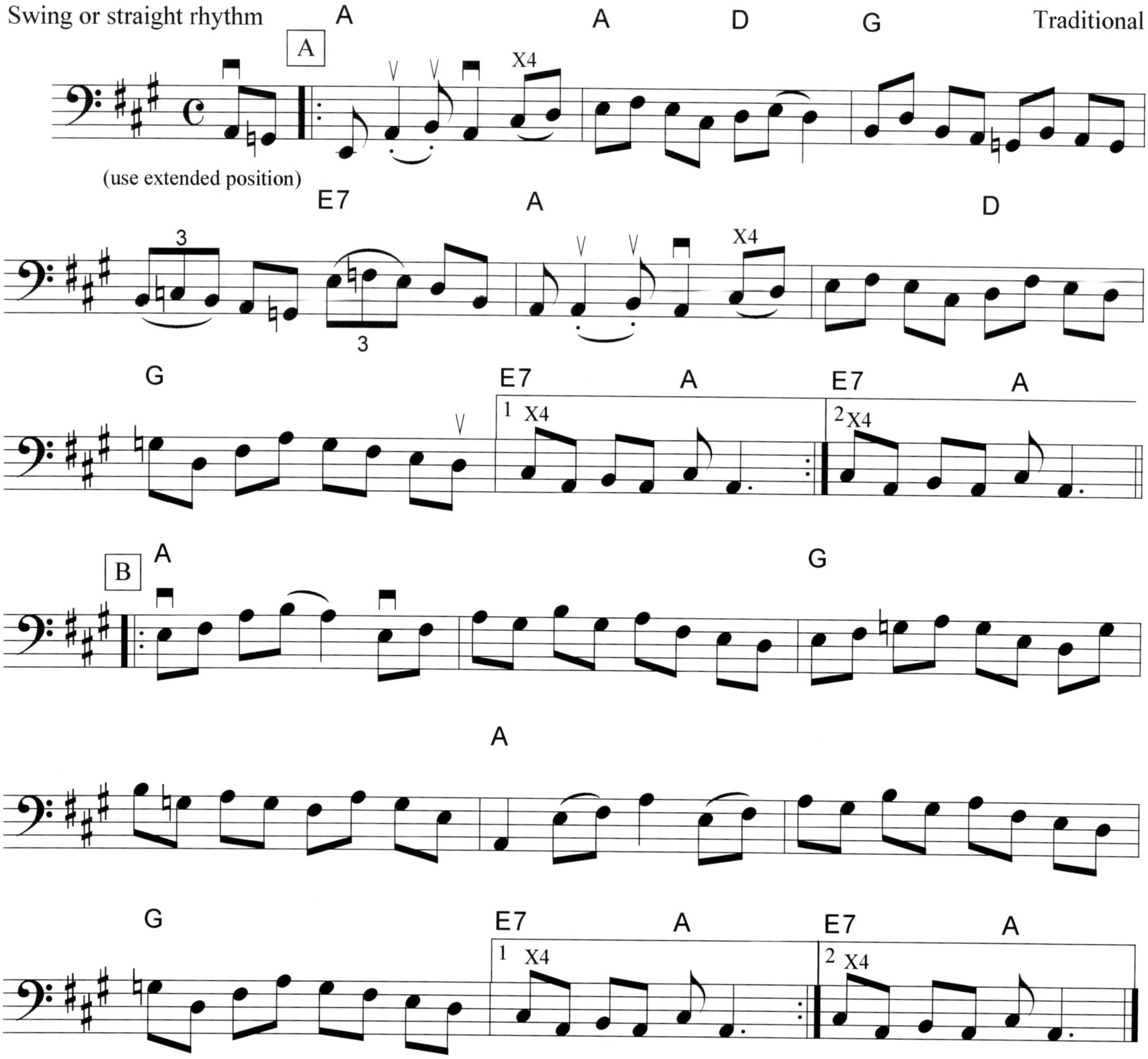


This tune is popular among bluegrass musicians as "Salt Creek". In a bluegrass setting it should be played at a fast tempo and a straight rhythm. Played as a Texas-style hoedown, "Salt River" should have more of a swing rhythm and a moderate tempo.

48

# Whiskey Before Breakfast

This version has been modified to simplify the fingering.

Swing rhythm
Fast or moderate tempo

Traditional

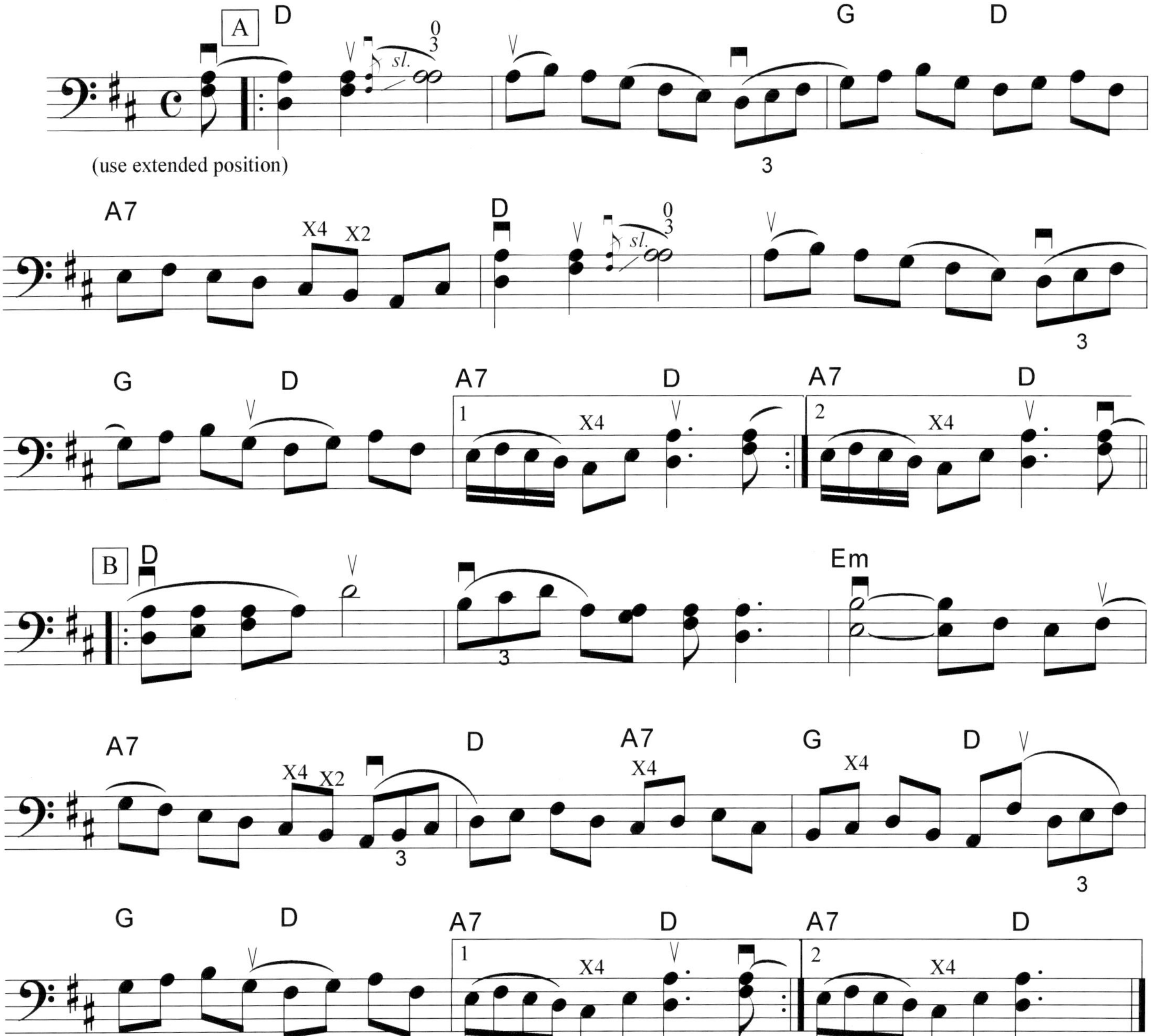

49

# Cattle in the Cane

This version is modified to simplify the fingering.

Swing rhythm
Fast or moderate tempo

Traditional

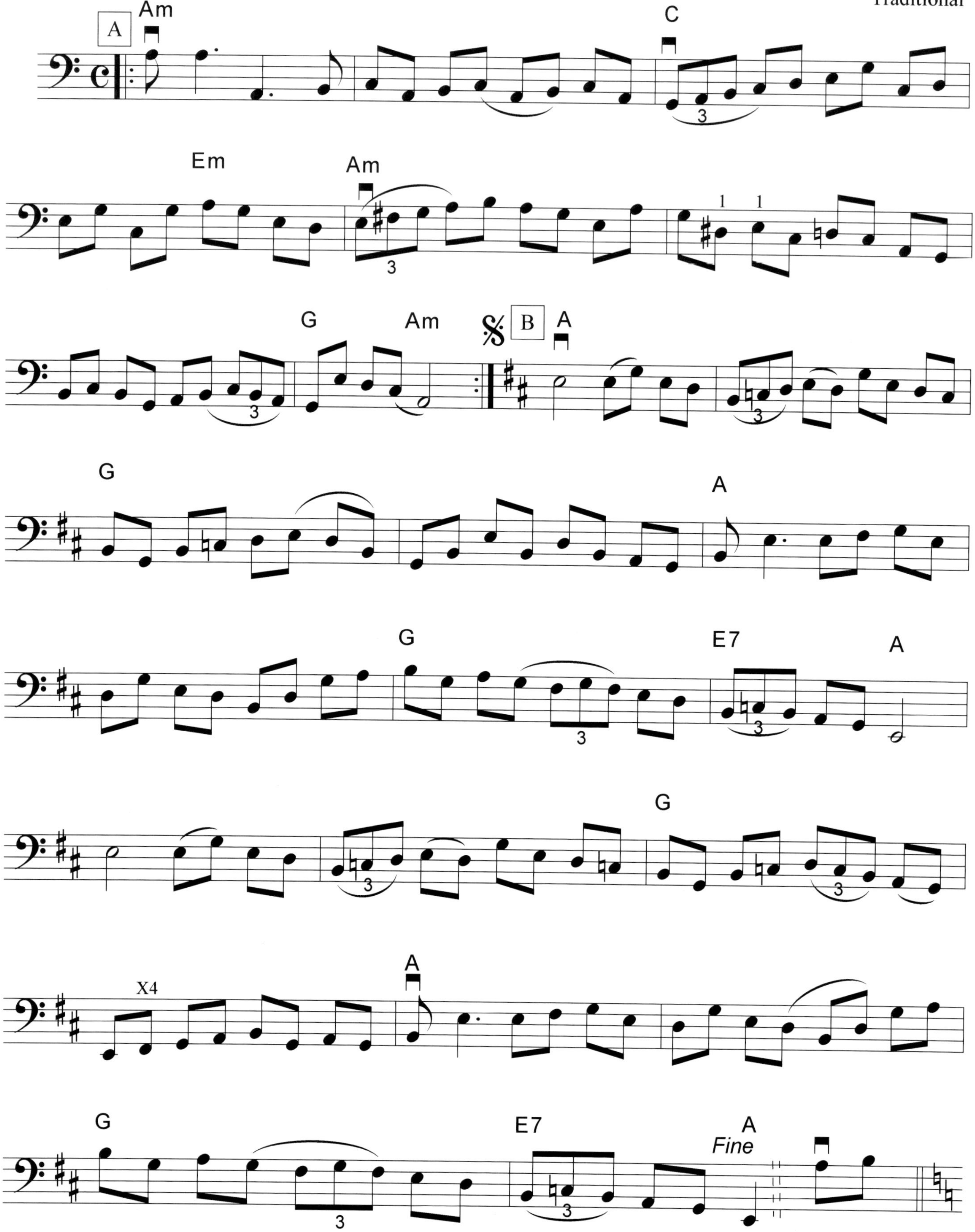

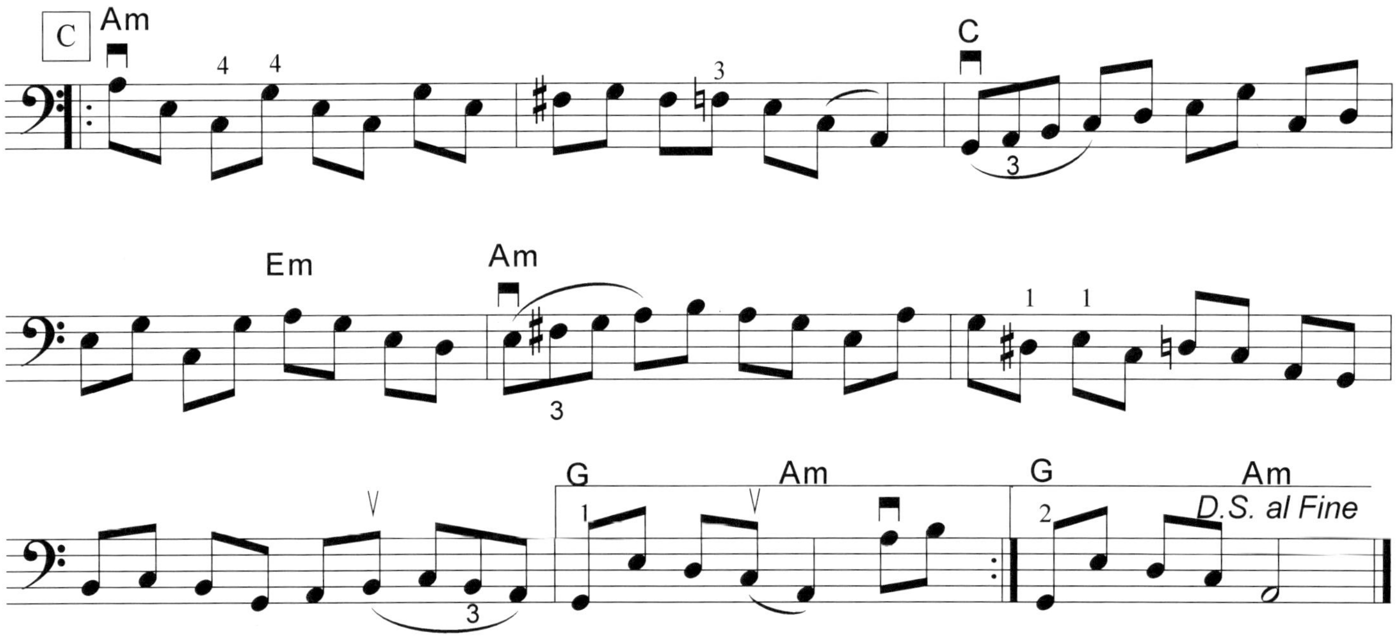


Traditionally, the A and B parts of this tune would be reversed.

50

# Black and White Rag

(Simplified)

This version has been modified to simplify the fingering.

Swing rhythm
Fast or moderate tempo

George Botsford

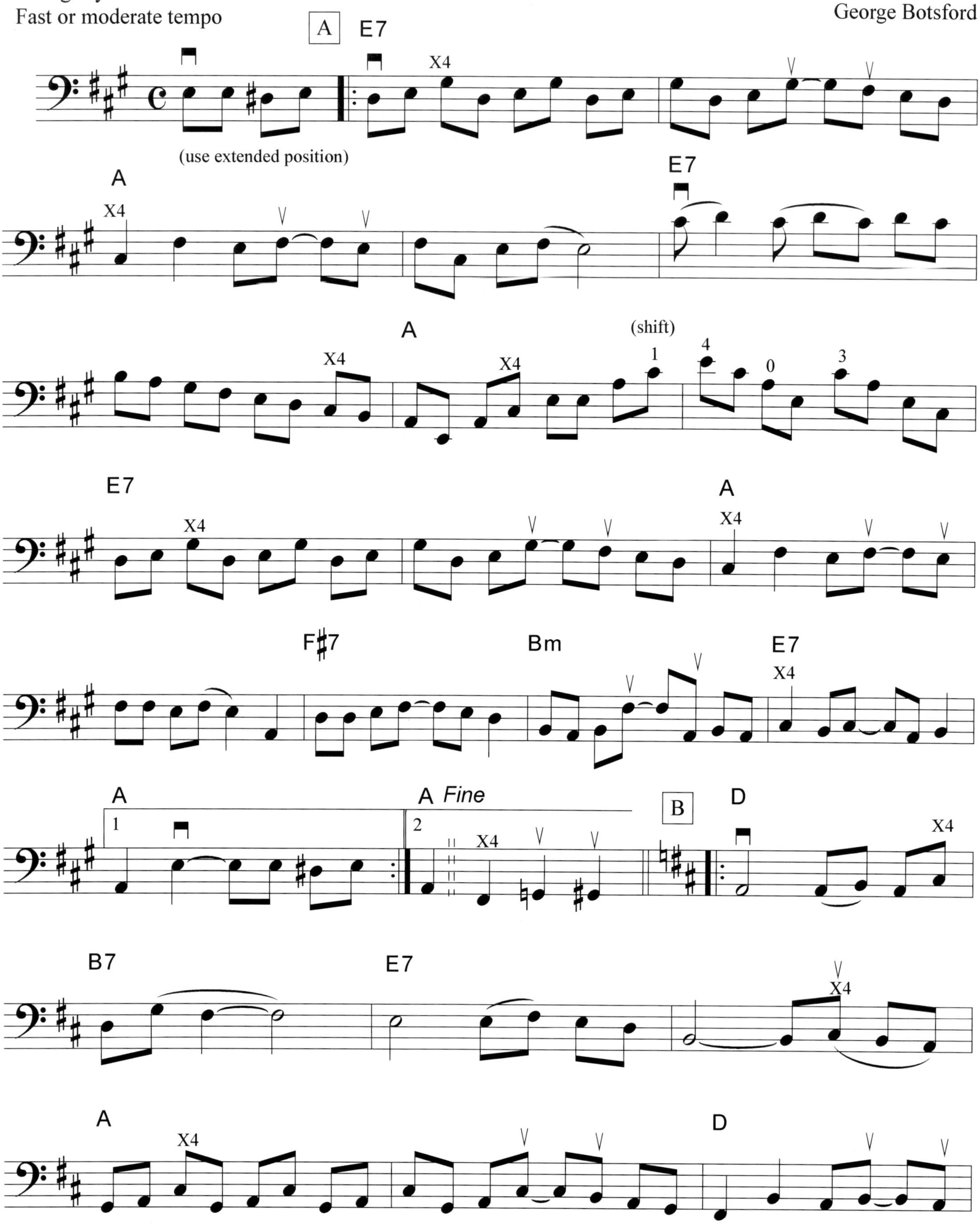

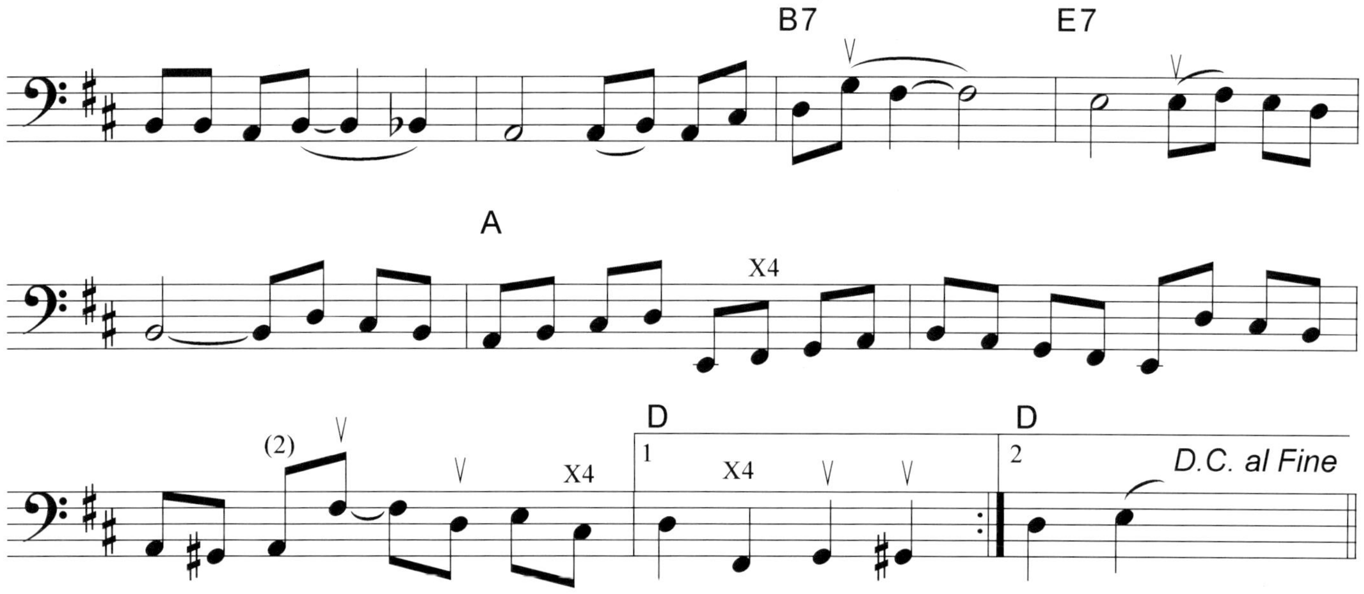
B7
E7
A
X4
(2)
X4
D
1
X4
D
2
D.C. al Fine

51

# Little Joe

This version has been modified to simplify the fingering.

Swing rhythm
Moderate tempo

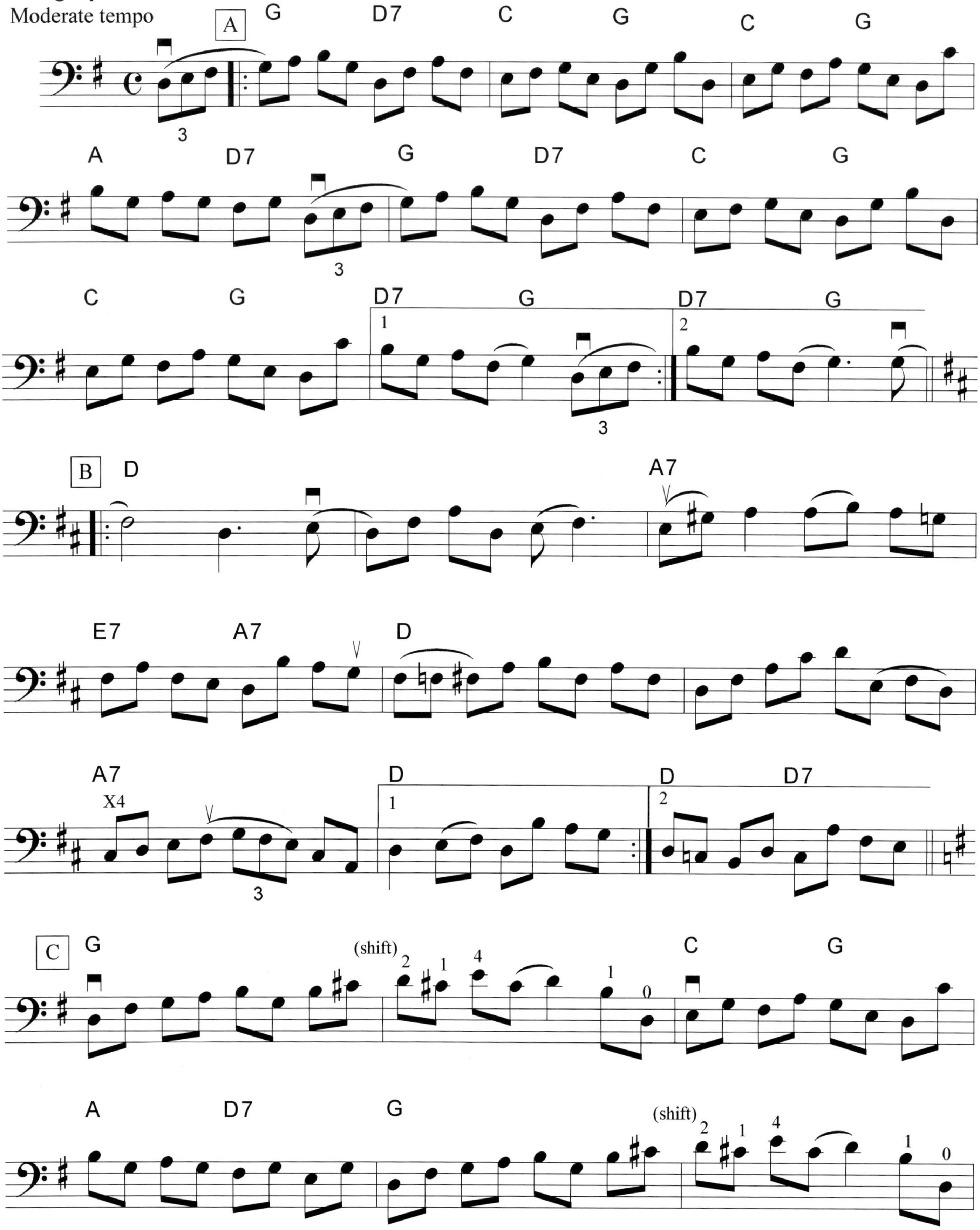

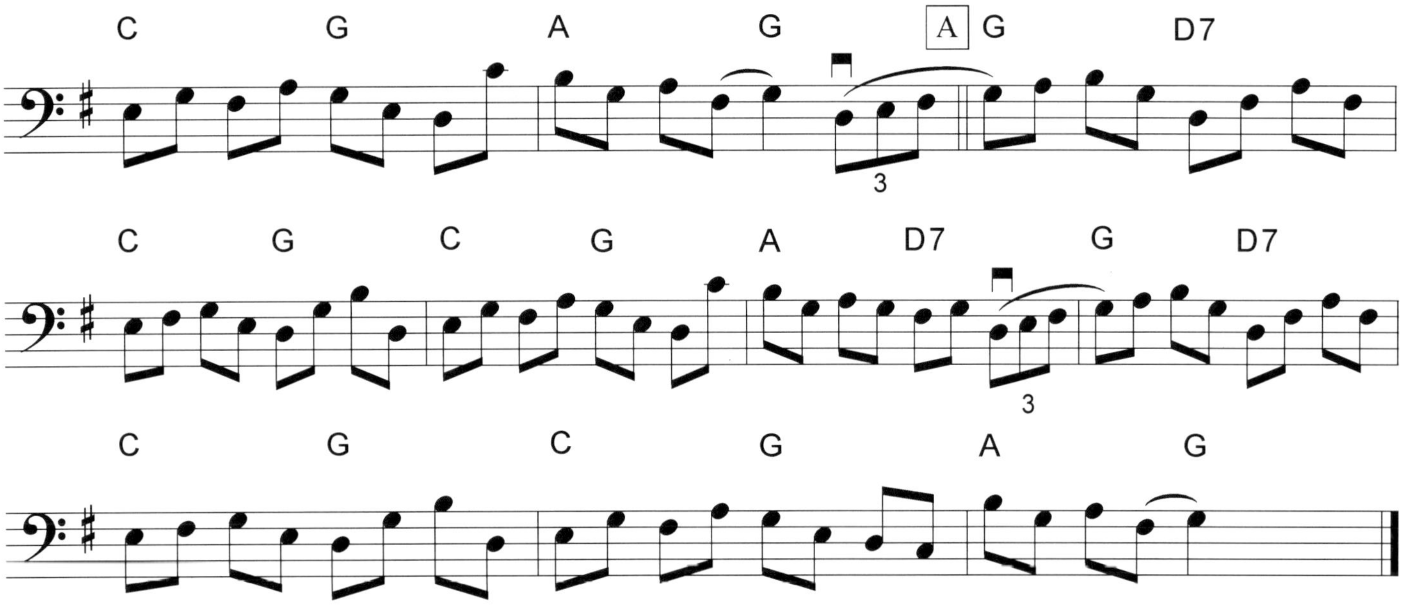
C G A G A G D7
3
C G C G A D7 G D7
3
C G C G A G